THE HALF THAT'S NEVER BEEN TOLD

THE HALF THAT'S NEVER BEEN TOLD

THE REAL-LIFE REGGAE ADVENTURES OF DOCTOR DREAD

BY DOCTOR DREAD

Published by Akashic Books
©2015 Doctor Dread

ISBN-13: 978-1-61775-290-2
Library of Congress Control Number: 2014938693

All rights reserved
First printing

Grateful acknowledgment is made for the right to reprint some of the lyrics to "It's Alright, Ma (I'm Only Bleeding)" by Bob Dylan on page 196 of this volume. Copyright ©1965 by Warner Bros. Inc.; renewed 1993 by Special Rider Music.

Akashic Books
Twitter: @AkashicBooks
Facebook: AkashicBooks
E-mail: info@akashicbooks.com
Website: www.akashicbooks.com

Livicated* to all those who help others and
are not only focused on their own self-betterment.

**I and I do not use the word "dedicated" as we choose instead to focus on life.*

TABLE OF CONTENTS

The truth is an offense, but not a sin . . .
—from "Jah Live" by Bob Marley & the Wailers

INTRODUCTION
BY BUNNY WAILER

I first met Doctor Dread in 1981 after the passing of my brother Robert Marley. This was around the time I released the *Rock 'n' Groove* album, ended my licensing and distribution relationship with Island Records/Chris Blackwell, and moved with my brethren in developing Cash and Carry Records. We developed a close relationship with Doctor Dread through his respect for the culture of Rastafari. He has been and still is a favorite brother of I, Bunny Wailer, apart from being a favorite distributor of the great reggae music, and also a producer of great standards.

Doctor Dread is one of the few international producers to travel to Jamaica and engage the singers and musicians not only in business, but also as a unique people of Jamaica. He bought a home in Portland to extend that relationship. So I have always had a good feeling about him as a person, not just taking out and away but giving back.

Doctor Dread has been a very serious contributor to the global value of this great reggae music. RAS Records has been and somehow still is the record label responsible for so many of the talents, including myself, who have been established coming from Jamaica—and his eloquence surrounding this great music is enormous.

Our relationship is built on a trust in consigning and licensing records and grew toward our most major project, that of the Bob Marley Hall of Fame box set, for which we won a Grammy. Outside of the record business that Doctor Dread eventually sold to Sanctuary Records in 2003, we established a publishing agreement that keeps us in business today.

Apart from being a serious businessman, Doctor Dread to I is a brother, a father figure of two sons, and a family man with his wife Debbie running the publishing arm. As a couple they work well together. Doctor Dread has also been my road manager on tours of great memories along with Count Ossie's band and Capleton, also several shows involving my nephews such as Ziggy, Steve, Ky-Mani, Julian, and Damian Marley (the Marley Clan). Doctor Dread once took us all to his home and we cooked a memorable feast.

During one of his most significant challenges related to his health, Doctor Dread reached out to me and we had many important reasonings on life where he deepened his faith in Rastafari.

Myself and Doc have never had any quarrel or financial problems working together for more than thirty years and even up until now, as he is still active as my publisher. Any difference of opinion has always been brought out in the open and worked through, such is the confidence of always aiming to do the right thing.

Doctor Dread, being true to himself, has moved on to producing and distributing food associated with the culture, and I know that whatever he is doing, he will be doing that which is beneficial and respectful to all that he has learned, taken, and given in his relationship to Jamaica and the Rastafari family. He has extended that relationship to Washington, DC, where he is often host to the Rastafari family in the Jamaican diaspora at times and events of significance.

I do hope that whatever is said of Doctor Dread and what he says of himself, that herein I have exalted a brother's relationship with I, Bunny Wailer.

One Love, One Heart, Let's Stay Together to Make Things Right. Yu heeeaar!

Hon. Neville O. Livingston O.J., C.D.
a.k.a. Bunny Wailer

FOREWORD

Forward ever, backward never . . .
—Rasta philosophy

I give thanks for what I consider to be such an extraordinary life full of incredible experiences, people, and manifestations of a reality that are all unique to I and I. It is truly a gift to have been given the opportunity and blessed by the Creator to turn my passion and love of reggae music, Rastafari, and Jamaican culture into a business that afforded me a life where I could support my family and travel to every corner of the Earth, meeting the most remarkable of men and women. I've also been granted the freedom to let my creative side be the force that has clearly guided me. While many people trod off to work each day and punch a time clock and have no real love for their jobs, and are only there to get a paycheck, I had the luxury of doing what I truly loved. A livity. My work became my life.

I believe that the creation of RAS (Real Authentic Sound) Records and Tafari Music (my publishing company) was a destiny that was set before I. And I and I must give thanks to the many artists and musicians who allowed me into their lives and who accepted me into their culture. The intimate relationships I have cultivated have been a remarkable inspiration for me. And the country of Jamaica has imbued within me a spirit that has greatly surpassed any feeling the country of my birth could have fed me. Imagine: A small little island in the Caribbean that gave rise to reggae music and the Rastafari way of life, both of which have reached to all parts of the Earth and had such a powerful influence on so many people from North America to Europe to Asia to Africa. Maybe it truly is the mythical Atlantis.

I never really had the intention of writing a book about my experiences, although I have been encouraged to do so by many people over the years. The main catalyst that triggered the desire to document my life was a book by Tad Hershorn entitled *Norman Granz: The Man Who Used Jazz for Justice*. I saw many similarities between this jazz producer's approach to music and the artists he worked with and my own. And knowing that a youth who worked for me at RAS when he was only sixteen years old and always exhibited a true passion for his work and whose integrity I always respected had started a small publishing company in New York which focused on Caribbean culture and writers, I decided to move forward with this project. Johnny Temple, the publisher of Akashic Books, has been a great inspiration for me. He has held onto his beliefs and not sold out to the corporate world but has instead chosen to maintain his freedom and keep his small, hard-working staff always reaching for their goals.

My approach to this book has been the same as how I would produce an album. Each chapter is a song. And I have layered them with different verses and choruses. Sometimes with a riff that is explosive and sometimes with a strum of tenderness. I have probably let a few skeletons escape from the closet and they are now dancing around out in the open. Maybe skanking down the street or just peering around a corner to see what is coming. If I have offended anyone, I do offer my apologies. My intention was only to let the truth be known from my own perspective.

(These days, a career in the music business is no longer a full-blown profession.) And although RAS Records clearly needed to make a profit to support myself and the artists and allow me to record albums that were not designed to make money but to expose a side of Jamaican culture, my alter ego—as my friend Dawn Bunetta described it—of Doctor Dread is still alive and well. (My birth name is Gary Himelfarb.)

A very important focus of my life now is with the Power of the Trinity. When it was explained to me that the Power of the Trinity referred to the Father, the Son, and the Holy Spirit, it gave me something to really think about. And as numbers and mathematics had played an important role in my life, I began to look for meaning in the number 3 and the power therein. The vocal harmony groups of reggae usually comprised three singers—Bob, Peter, and Bunny together as Wailers being the most famous example. Since I have always believed there is a guiding force (God), and the explanation of mere coincidence does not often resonate within me, I looked for more meaning. Always seeking enlightenment. And in my life, the Power of the Trinity has come to mean that Jesus was the greatest man to ever walk the face of this Earth, that Haile Selassie I is the second coming of Jesus, and that Bob Marley is the prophet. That's just how it is for me. Powerfully. I'm not saying or suggesting it needs to or should be that way for anyone else. But it is for me. And I try my best every day to measure up to their words and examples of how they lived their lives while here on Earth.

And through all the trials and tribulations I have faced, I believe that I have reached a state of what I loosely describe as nirvana. I am now ready and prepared and have no fear of entering the hereafter. I do not look upon death as something negative. I am comfortable with its inevitably and know it is part of all our destinies. Part of life. Moving forward forever.

I also must, although I have been asked not to, give thanks to my family. I am so lucky to be married to the finest person I have ever known in my lifetime, and to have been blessed with two wonderful sons. They say the gift of God is eternal life, and I have always believed that this means to spawn descendents who will carry forth your spirit and pass this on to their children, and so on.

Jah guide and protect you all, and remember to keep moving forward. Forever.

Raspect,

Doctor Dread

GREGORY ISAACS

Beef deh a market, marrow in a bone.
What don't concern you, please leave it alone . . .
—Gregory Isaacs, from "Mr. Cop"

It was sometime between two and three a.m. and I was working at Gussie Clarke's Music Works Studio that had relocated from Slipe Road to Windsor Road in uptown Kingston, Jamaica. I was in the large new room Gussie had built, voicing an artist for one of my *Reggae for Kids* projects. I always liked to work in the studio from around eight p.m. till the early-morning hours as I believed the creative juices would flow best for both me and the musicians, and once locked away in a studio there is no day or night. Just the creative vibe of music. I was always completely blown away by the evolution of music: from silence grew note after note which eventually would end up as a song.

Someone entered the room and announced, "Doctor Dread, Gregory is out in the waiting room and he wants to see you." My relationship with Gregory went back to the early '80s when he had a small record shop on Chancery Lane in downtown Kingston. I had released a number of his CDs and had produced a full album and many individual tracks as well. I was also his music publisher, and I represented him in this regard on a worldwide basis. After Bob Marley, Gregory is the most popular artist to ever come out of Jamaica. And with a prolific body of work that is unparalleled within reggae music.

Gregory, looking disheveled in a white tank top and weaving from side to side, turned to me and said, "Me vex with you, Doctor Dread. You no do me right." And when I observed him a little closer I noticed he was pointing a small two-barrel, pearl-coated pistol at me. An antique-looking type of thing. There were a bunch of people in the room and everyone was just sitting still and observing the situation. I knew Gregory was wasted on crack cocaine, as he had been smoking it daily for over twenty years. No one could understand how he had managed to survive this long, but I think I knew his secret. I looked at him and asked what the problem was— I was actually more concerned that the gun would go off accidentally; I was not so worried that he was mad enough to actually shoot me.

"Me need money, Doctor Dread," he said. "You collect all this money for me but me nah get enough."

Gregory could go through money pretty quick. He took care of lots of people from Jamaica to England and had a serious crack habit to feed. Yes, some people may have considered him a thug from the ghetto, but he had a heart of gold and always looked after those around him. And his million-dollar voice certainly earned him

millions of dollars. When Gregory would moan the ladies would swoon. And if the women love an artist the
men will surely follow to stay closer to the women. That
is just how it works.

He always used to say to me, "You know me love
you, Doctor Dread, but me love money just a likkle bit
more!" And then he would let out a laugh. And when I
paid him he would always ask for me to "put a likkle
fertilizer on it to make it grow." Or call me and tell me
his "reservoir is dry" and he needed to see some rain
come down. He was one of a kind. A one-horse race.
No one could compete with him. Dennis Brown tried
but could not keep up and passed away from trying too
hard.

I got to know Gregory and his wife June very well.
I remember one night I was working at Tuff Gong studios on Hope Road. This is where Bob Marley lived and
recorded many of his albums. Back in the day they allowed certain people to record there and I was afforded
that privilege. The vibes in the place were really special,
and I was working on a Michigan & Smiley album when
Gregory drove into the yard in his BMW model 2002.
"Doctor Dread, I need your help. Some people are looking for me and I need you to drive me out of here. I am
going to slump down in the seat so them can't see me.
Just drop me off in New Kingston and I will pay for you
to take a taxi back to the studio."

"Gregory, can't you see I am busy working?"

"Doctor Dread, I really need your help. You just got
to help me."

How could I say no? I had everyone take a break and
drove Gregory into New Kingston. I later realized what

a fool I had been—if someone saw Gregory's car and was looking for him, they could have shot me instead. In Kingston after dark, gunshots are not uncommon. When I thought about it later I just had to smile. *Gregory, you no easy.*

I recorded the album *Pardon Me!* with Gregory when he and Dean Fraser and the 809 Band had just completed a US tour. Gregory often had trouble getting into the US. I guess he had a pretty serious criminal record, but I really do not know for sure. I just accepted him as Gregory. In fact, that is how I get along with most people. I just try to accept them for who they are: I take the good with the bad. Only Jah is perfect, so the rest of us can simply try to do our best. This is how I have managed to get along with some very eccentric people whose creativity can take them to some extremely faraway places. Gregory was one of the three true geniuses I came into contact with in all my years of being in the reggae business, and I had a great deal of respect for him and his far-out ways.

After recording this album for me, Gregory decided to stay in Washington, DC, for a while with his wife June. He would move from hotel to hotel for about one week at a time. Licking the crack pipe hard! He had this one that looked like a bong and I knew it was a major instrument when Gregory was looking to do some serious freebasing. I remember getting up one morning at five and writing a bio for Gregory to use at his shows, and to go out as a press release with the new album I had produced. After reading it Gregory looked at me and said, "Boy, Doctor Dread, you really know me." I was able to articulate who Gregory was and make reference to his outlaw character without spilling all the beans. I think he appreciated that. I knew he was using crack to try to dull his very finely tuned brain and to separate him from a world of conflicts and demands. He told me women would come to his room after his shows and not leave. Just stay there all night until he had to kick them out, or he'd get so wasted they would leave. Everyone wanted to get close to Gregory, and he used the drug to keep them away.

I could sense his difficulty in dealing with his stardom. I had arranged for him to go to a drug treatment center in Pennsylvania to try to get rid of his crack habit. The plan was for me to drive him up and he would stay there until he was clean and free of the shit. Many big rock stars had gone there and it was not cheap, but I was willing to pay for it because I believed it could help him. I came that next morning to pick him up and he had obviously been up all night seriously licking his pipe. The big one. He and June were ready to kill each other and Gregory told me to get the fuck out of there. That he was not going anywhere. I called the doctor at the retreat and explained the situation, and I then realized that people are not ready to get help until THEY are ready. It is not up to others to get them the help. They have to *want* it. And Gregory was certainly not there yet.

I remember another time when I had Gregory in Lion and Fox Studios in downtown DC. Gregory had done a wonderful version of "Puff the Magic Dragon" for my first of many *Reggae for Kids* CDs. He really nailed it. I had lined him up for doing "Day-O," a song popularized by Harry Belafonte that was originally sung by the workers on the north coast of Jamaica in the 1920s as they loaded bananas onto boats bound for England. It was an easy enough tune, and I already had the rhythm completed, so all Gregory had to do was voice it. He came in and his jaw was moving back and forth. I had seen him like this many times and had assumed it was because he was really high. He went into the studio to voice the tune and he was so off-key I had to rewind the tape again and again. He just could not get it and I didn't understand why. It was an easy song and he was Gregory Isaacs. He said he needed a break and sent Peter Broggs, another Jamaican singer, out to the streets to score him some crack. After he smoked it up I noticed his jaw quit moving around. And when he went back into the studio he sang that song so beautifully you could have sworn it was his own. Perfect.

It was then I sadly realized he was a true addict. When addicts don't have their stuff they are not right. Not normal. Once they get it they become normal again. I really felt for him and knew what a struggle his life must have been, despite his success. He was comfortable enough around me to smoke his crack openly and I never put him down for it. Like I say, I just accepted it.

Gregory also had a softer side. He was once in my office at RAS while in DC and we were hanging out. Jim Fox had given me this big jar of atomic fireballs as a Christmas present. In Jamaica, because the currency is so undervalued, when you go to buy things at the supermarket you sometimes get a small handful of hard candy as change. These are known as "sweeties" and Jamaicans bring them home and give them to their kids. I asked Gregory if he would like a sweetie and handed him one of the fireballs. He put it in his mouth and was talking to me and I noticed after a while that he was starting to shift around as the heat from the fireball finally started busting loose in his mouth. I was having a hard time keeping a straight face and when it got to the point that he could no longer take the heat, he took it from his mouth and shouted at me, "Bloodclot, Doctor Dread! You a burn up me mouth!" I laughed so hard I fell out of the fucking chair. I am lucky he never kicked me while I was down on the ground writhing in laughter. But we could joke around like that, we were comfortable with each other.

When I was in Jamaica recently, June reminded me of the time I was in their hotel room in DC during a hurricane and a large tree snapped in half outside the window. For some reason Gregory and I decided to wrestle to see who was stronger. I threw him down and some of his dreadlocks came out of his head. I made a joke about how I was going to put them in the Reggae Music Hall of Fame or sell them on eBay. Some kind of bullshit. June reminded me that he trimmed his locks shortly thereafter in Washington, DC, and when he returned to Jamaica to perform on the *Heineken Startime* show, the whole country was amazed to see Gregory without his dreadlocks.

Another time, I had him scheduled to do "Mr. Tambourine Man" for the Bob Dylan reggae album I was working on. I had gone to London to record him and J.C. Lodge, and my good friend the Mad Professor had let me book out his Ariwa studio on the outskirts of London, a pretty far ride from where both Gregory and J.C. were living at the time. I would generally record the rhythm tracks in advance, and would just need the singers to come after that and voice the tune. Later, I would over-dub harmonies, synthesizers, percussion, and horns. I had my formula pretty set, usually recording my albums in Kingston and mixing them in Washington, DC, with Jim Fox. J.C. came and did her tune and we waited for Gregory to arrive. He was scheduled for ten p.m. By midnight he had not shown up and the engineer wanted to leave, but I said to just wait. I knew he would come. At one a.m. he finally showed up. And when a Jamaican shows up late they usually do not apologize. They just greet you like everything is okay. It is a cultural thing and I had gotten used to it. In Jamaica they say "soon come," and that means that eventually it will happen. To just be patient. If you ever go to Jamaica and try to rush things too much, it will often backfire on you. You just gotta learn to relax and go with the flow. To chill. I was excited to have Gregory do this song. I felt he was like a modern-day Mr. Bojangles, and the song and he were very symbiotic. And I knew the line that says *"Take me disappearing through the smoke rings of my mind"* would resonate with Gregory. I was sure he could relate to that.

It took him many hours to voice that song. We had to punch him in line after line till he got it right. As a producer I would never accept anything less than the best an artist was capable of, and I really pushed Gregory hard that night. Yes, he took some breaks from the vocal booth to regain his composure. Between takes, he would step out pouring sweat, laugh, then say, "Boy, Doctor Dread, you a really work me hard tonight." But the proof is in the pudding. Gregory gave this his personal touch and I felt like I had gotten what I had bargained for.

I had him voice "House of the Rising Sun" earlier for the *Pardon Me!* album, and both these songs had a pure Gregory vibe to them once they were done.

So back to the incident in the studio with Gregory pointing that pistol at me. We talked it out and he eventually left, and the next week his brother called me from England and apologized profusely for what Gregory had done. But it never really changed anything between us. I was just glad the gun didn't accidentally go off. It was one story I did not bother to share with my family at the time, as I didn't want them to worry about my many trips to Kingston and all my late nights recording in the studios there. And Gregory and I never discussed that incident again and just went about our normal relationship like it never happened.

Gregory passed away in 2010 at the age of only fifty-nine years young. A doctor in England had found a spot on his lung, but he never got it looked after and he just grew weaker and weaker until he passed. I was asked to be a pallbearer at his funeral, which was a great honor. My wife Deb and I went to Jamaica and there was a big tribute concert held at the Ranny Williams Center in Kingston with many of Jamaica's top reggae artists performing. Deb and I were reunited with friends and artists we had worked with over the years and we could really feel the love and appreciation people had for us. When Jamaica gets into your soul it is for-iver and a blessed feeling. And it really is the people that make it such a blessed place.

I miss Gregory, and Tafari Music still represents his music publishing on a worldwide basis. He was unique.

One of a kind, and there will never be another like him. Rest in peace, my brother.

OH, JAMAICA

Oh, Jamaica. Oh, Jamaica. Oh, Jamaica.
You're always on my mind . . .
—Jimmy Cliff

After getting a serious dose of reggaemylitis when I first heard *The Harder They Come* in 1972 and Bob Marley's *Catch a Fire* the following year, I was determined to take a trip to Jamaica. I had been living off and on in South America for a few years and was quite accustomed to the tropical way of life. And the island that gave birth to both reggae and Rastafari was an intriguing, not-so-distant destination that I and I knew awaited I. My friend Steve Berman had been there and told me about a little beach town called Negril. He said I could walk from the airport in Montego Bay into town and find a place to stay, then figure out a way to get over to Negril. I was taking a black-and-white photography course at the Corcoran School of Art at the time and had met a dread there who told me about a guesthouse where I could stay in Montego Bay.

When everything finally came together in 1977 and it was time for me to go, the *Washington Post* had a front-page story warning people to stay away from Jamaica; the political turmoil had erupted into the streets and the island was not safe. Some friends and family encouraged me to postpone my trip but I decided to leave things in the hands of God. Mentally and spiritually I had been focusing on this trip and there was no turning back. I had planned to stay a few months but was not sure. All I really knew was that I could walk into MoBay from the airport, that there was a guesthouse I could check out, and from there, a hotel in Negril named Perseverance where I could stay for ten bucks a night. And I had the names of a few dreads there who I could check in with. I was all set.

I flew out of Baltimore into Montego Bay on Air Jamaica. I had very long hair and a long beard. And I was smoking lots of ganja at the time. Get the picture? I breezed through customs and as soon as I left the airport I threw away my two-week visitor-visa document they had given me to present upon my departure back to the States. Yes, I walked with my backpack into town taking in all the sights and sounds of this island paradise that is simultaneously blessed with its rich, vibrant culture and cursed in other ways I would soon discover. When I arrived at the guesthouse I was told, "We have never rented to a white man before but I see no reason why it should be a problem." I settled into my room, easily found some ganja, and as I was burning my first spliff in Jamaica I could hear Bob Marley in the distance: "*Hear the words of the Rastaman say: Babylon you throne gone down, gone down . . .*" I knew I had truly reached Jamaica.

I ended up walking through Green Island on my way to Negril. I had bought a red, gold, and green tam to cover my head and had my trusty backpack with me. A dread approached me and asked what it was I was looking to do. We reasoned for a while and he took a pin from his shirt that had a picture of Selassie I and the words *Sons of God*. He put this into my tam and blessed me and I was on my way again. I still have this pin in a Kangol hat I wear and it means a lot to me. It may have been what began my conversion into Rastafari.

I arrived in Negril and was amazed at the beauty of this place. A seven-mile stretch of white-sand beach with the gentle, clear green waters gracing its lovely shore. It was paradise. With thatch-roofed huts and coconut palms lining the beach, it had not yet exploded into the popular tourist destination it has now become. It was so laid-back and chill that it was like I had just fallen into a soft, comfy pillow and could let my conscience completely relax. I rented a small hut at Perseverance for ten dollars a night and became friendly with the staff there. I told them that my plan was to stay for a month. That I wanted to get to know Jamaica.

My shower was from a cold water pipe outside surrounded by some plants for privacy. No air conditioner but I did have electricity. And Dollie and Jules would sometimes cook food and invite me over to eat with them. Across the road on the beach side were some dreads I got to know, and we would sit around a bonfire at night burning spliffs and talking. Negril and Westmoreland Parish had earned the reputation for having the best weed in Jamaica, and they were serious about the good sinse they cultivated there. One night as we were sitting around the fire, a brethren brought me some cornmeal porridge. I thought about the Bob Marley song "No Woman No Cry" where he says, *"And then Georgie would make the fire light, log wood burnin' through the night. Then we would cook cornmeal porridge, of which I'll share with you."* It brought tears to my eyes. Being on the beach at night, reasoning with my brethren, and sharing in the cornmeal porridge. The Jamaica I had experienced in the songs of reggae was a reality that I was becoming completely absorbed in.

I was hungry. Hungry for knowledge. Hungry to learn as much as I could about the culture and people of Jamaica. I let my hair go and it began to knot up. ("Dread natty dreadlocks.") During the day I would hang on the beach or walk around the place, and at night I would either be with my friends or hanging out in my hut. I had an excellent road map of Jamaica I had gotten from an Esso station and I began to study it. I knew I wanted to experience other parts of the island but was not sure where I would go. People told me to stay out of Kingston; it was dangerous and there was no real reason for me to go there. One night while perusing the map in my hut, I spotted a small area called Fruitful Vale. It was in the parish of Portland and not too far from Blue Mountain Peak. Blue Mountain Peak, at 7,402 feet, is the highest elevation in Jamaica. Fruitful Vale sounded like a magical place to me. Maybe paradise. So I decided that is where I would go.

For me, it was all about vibes. I just went with what my spirit told me I should do and knew that somehow along the way I would figure things out. On the map I noticed there was a train line from Montego Bay to

Kingston that had a spur that went over to Port Antonio. I heard that travel by train in Jamaica was quite an experience and people even sat on top of the train and that it was a wild ride. Just what the doctor ordered. So my backpack and I got on that train and off we went. I decided to get off in the coastal town of Old Harbour. This is a small town where the ladies sit out on the street and sell fried fish and bammy from these glass cases. It is still the same all these years later. Fish and bammy. And I am not sure of the reason why, but I decided I would walk from Old Harbour to Bog Walk. Now this is quite a long trip and I think it may have taken me a few weeks. Just me and my backpack walking across the island of Jamaica. This has become somewhat legendary as some Jamaicans cannot believe a person could walk that distance.

People along the way would say I could catch a ride but I told them it was a nice day and I just preferred to walk. They would invite me into their homes and offer me fresh lemonade and talk to me about what I was doing. In truth, this is how I really got to know Jamaica and its people. At night I might sleep under some grapefruit trees or find a room in a house. Sometimes cold ground was my bed at night. But I was okay. I was absorbing the vibe and spirit of Jamaica. I just took my time and walked and rested when I needed to rest.

By the time I got to Bog Walk I was exhausted. My backpack was falling apart and as I sat in a bar having lunch I took out my map and saw that the train went through Bog Walk over to Port Antonio. So I put my plan to keep walking across Jamaica on hiatus and took in the sights and sounds by train once more till I reached Hope Bay.

Upon arriving there I inquired if there were any ho-tel rooms available. I was told there were no rooms in town but that Mr. Maxie, who had a place right across from the train station, rented out rooms. I checked with Mr. Maxie and he said he did have a room I could rent. No electricity and a shared bathroom but I guess that would have to do. Mr. Maxie was an older man and he would sit on his porch and sell individual cigarettes. I started to make some friends in town and told them of my plan to go up to Fruitful Vale. They explained that there was no town there, just some verdant valleys and that it was very rural. Most of my days were spent in town at a local bar checking out all the amazing music they had on the jukebox and drinking ginger beer. Or I would go and hang out with Dreadie, the local ganja dealer who lived right in town—everyone including the police knew he sold ganja but they just left him alone as he was a peaceful man who wasn't hurting anyone.

I would also venture to the outskirts of town to a place called Somerset Falls where I would bathe and swim and commune with nature. It was a beautiful spot far off the beaten track. It was like my private paradise. I would swim through the falls there into a cave I dubbed "Creation," as it had many nubs and rocks shaped by centuries of water that reminded me of a womb. I would sit in there and meditate and think about life. In Cre-ation. At night I would burn my kerosene lamp and read in my room.

I loved the peace and quiet of Hope Bay. I just had my simple routine of going out to Somerset Falls in the mornings and chilling back in town for the day with an occasional trip into Port Antonio. There was a great bakery there (the Coronation Bakery) where they had still-warm hard-dough bread for sale as it came out fresh right from the oven. And we used the paper they wrapped the bread in to build our spliffs, as rolling paper (or Rizlas, as Jamaicans would call them) was scarce and hard to find. It was harsh on the throat but it's what everyone used in that time.

The produce market there was also excellent, as Portland is known as the lushest of all the parishes in Jamaica due to the fact it gets so much rain from the clouds hovering over the Blue Mountains. And just like in South America before, I was interested in all the different types of fruits and vegetables and herbs and whatever Jah had put on this Earth for the use of mankind. So I got friendly with the women in the market and was always finding out about different kinds of produce. Soursop, sweet sop, custard apple. All of the same family but each with a subtle taste and different use. And if you've ever had soursop ice cream I am sure you know what I mean. I even got my first "stinkin' toe" there—I busted it open with my shoe, and when I tasted it the fruit turned my whole mouth dry and I almost died from not being able to breathe. Singer Freddie McGregor told me he used to eat these as a kid growing up in Clarendon, and Bunny Wailer would mix them with honey and make something you could eat that must have had its origins from biblical times. But I would never again try eating one on its own.

One day I decided to finally venture up to Fruitful Vale and see what it was all about. Small roads took me higher and higher into the mountains. But it was just an area. Nothing to distinguish it from the land across the way. So I decided to continue up the roads to Blue Mountain Peak, asking people for directions along the way. As I climbed higher the road became a narrow path up to the peak. It was very hot and the walk was fairly strenuous. I came to a small stream (the original Carib Indian name for Jamaica is *Xamayca*; it means "land of wood and water" and is a testament to the abundance of fresh water in Jamaica compared to other islands in the Caribbean) and decided I would take a break and have some food from my backpack. After bathing in the stream and resting on a rock I noticed a big old fat psilocybin mushroom growing right next to the water. Just like the ones I had picked in South America. I knew it had been put there by the Almighty Jah and that it was there for me to consume. As I relaxed by the stream and ate my lunch along with that one big mushroom, I reflected upon my life and my recent experiences in Jamaica. Then, as I continued climbing again, the effects of the mushroom began to take effect.

I had been told there was a coffee plantation just below the peak where campers would spend the night before making their final ascent. It was owned by an Englishman named Mr. Algrove and was reputed to grow some of the finest Blue Mountain coffee in the world.

As I reached the coffee plantation just before the sunset I was in a very high state of mind. Some dreads there ran me a hot bath through this wood stove, and while I kicked back in the tub, I burned a big spliff and listened to JBC radio. They announced that Count Ossie had passed away that day and they were featuring music from Count Ossie and the Mystic Revelation of Rastafari. The record *Grounation* is a landmark three-LP set that blends Afro-Cuban jazz with reggae and roots. And like the three-LP set from George Harrison (a former member of a supergroup from the '60s and '70s whose name I cannot quite remember), *All Things Must Pass*, this release became a blueprint for my life. I don't know why. It just happened that way. Possibly, again, through the Power of the Trinity.

The next morning I rose early to make my final five-hour trek up to the top. The pinnacle. The highest point in Jamaica. My plan was to sleep up there in a shelter I was told had been constructed for hikers. I also planned to fast and just meditate and soar over the valleys like an eagle. The view was spectacular. It is said you can see ninety miles to Cuba from there, and I do believe I caught a glimpse of it when the clouds cleared. I was in the clouds, above the clouds. I felt good to be there without another person all day and night.

My fasting put me into a good place, and in my meditation I realized that when Moses went to the top of Mount Sinai, he most likely fasted for forty days and nights, and through his spiritual awakening he came up with the Ten Commandments. Of course it was inspired by the connection he had made with God, though I do not believe God actually handed him tablets carved in stone. But I do believe that God gave him the inspiration to carve them. And like others after him, like Nelson Mandela who would go on hunger fasts to protest injustice, I was sure that Moses too reached a very high state of overstanding.

I think it was Galileo who said, "What goes up must come down," so the next day I descended from the mountaintop feeling quite exalted from my day and night in solitude—and at least I wasn't carrying any carved stone tablets. Eventually the path came out high up in the mountains to a place known as Hagley Gap. The splendor of the Blue Mountains was all around me and I was taking it in: The smells of pine and eucalyptus. The fires being lit by the mountain residents to cook their food. The sounds of birds and insects. It was a harmonious, peaceful place and I came to realize that I had in fact reached Fruitful Vale. That it was all around me, and that a name is just a label for something, and that Fruitful Vale was as much of a concept as it was a place.

I made it back to my digs at Maxie's house in Hope Bay and settled into my room after my mountain adventure. I was beginning to feel as though my time in this part of Jamaica had been fulfilled, so I headed back to Negril, where I met up with my friend Bongo. I had amassed a great selection of 45 rpm vinyl from my travels across the island, my hair was all matted up in dreadlocks, and Bongo's wife Fanette arranged for me to spin one night at a cool club on the beach. We had a blast that evening, and the pleasure I got from seeing people's reactions to the music I was playing was a precursor to my stint as a disc jockey, when I took on the name Doctor Dread and would spin on the radio those very same records I had discovered many years earlier.

But my maiden sojourn to Jamaica was coming to an end. I had learned quite a bit about the country and its people and felt at ease there. When I arrived at the airport and the immigration officer asked for a copy of my tourist visa, I acted incredulous and pretended I did not have any idea what he was referring to. He then looked in my passport and gasped when he saw I had been in Jamaica for over three months. He started to get disturbed but I offered a big smile and told him what a beautiful country he had, and how grateful I was for the opportunity to get to know the place. He shook his head and laughed before stamping my passport.

Upon arrival back at my parents' house in Washington, DC, my mom grabbed my natty hair and asked me if I had bubble gum in there. It made no sense to try to explain what I was feeling so I took off with a girlfriend shortly thereafter and we hitchhiked down to Florida. Down to Tarpon Springs where Greek fisherman used to dive for sponges with those old brass helmets on their heads. We got hired to pick oranges and I think we may have been the only white folks out there working. And even though those wooden ladders were rickety and the thorns of the orange trees would scrape up our arms, we had to fill a big bucket before we got paid our measly little salary each day. At night we ate tzatziki and drank retsina wine. And we ate a lot of oranges and laughed. We then hitchhiked out to Texas to spend some time with Kim's brother in Houston. We got picked up by someone named James, who had a gun in his glove compartment and insisted the three of us sleep in the same hotel room that night in a king-size bed. Nothing bad happened, and Kim and I still laugh about that night driving across the country with James. It's funny the little things you never forget.

Houston was not the vibe for me. I still had my dreadlocks and wore a multicolored poncho I had bought in Ecuador. The poncho was also good as a blanket at night when sleeping out under the stars. And in fact I still have it. One night some cops approached me. When I saw them coming I stuffed my bag of weed down my pants. Maybe they were not used to seeing a dread-locked, bearded dude wearing a multicolored poncho in their (red) neck of the woods. Stupid me; I had not realized I wasn't wearing underwear and that bag of weed slid right down my leg and onto the ground just as they were searching me. I exclaimed, "That's not mine! How did that get there?" They had probably heard that one once or twice before. They booked me and took me to the station and it was then that I decided I had to get out of Texas.

I would have to return there to face the charges, but in the interim I flew back home to DC and decided to cut off my hair and shave off my beard so I would not be such an obvious target for Babylon. To make myself more invisible. To become a sheep in wolf's clothing. Some people grow dreadlocks, yet I realized I would be most effective in fighting Babylon by flying under the radar. But first, since I was going to shave off my five-year-old beard anyway, I thought I might as well just shave one half and then remove the other half the next day. Just for kicks. I decided I would go out on the town and try to pick up chicks. Like some girl would even consider going home with a total maniac with one half of a beard. I hit a few bars looking for girls but instead got totally wasted on some 151-proof rum, and when I came back to my house late that night my dad was in the kitchen with a bunch of his construction buddies playing cards. I was belligerent and very drunk and I had half a fucking beard. I insisted they let me in on the game. My poor father. I was told the next day that I had become extremely aggressive with everyone at the table, vomited all over the kitchen, and passed out. My parents must have been so proud of me: a half-bearded loco who had been living on the edge for quite some time now. I decided I did not want to put my parents through any more stress, and started to clean myself up. It's a bit of a haze, but maybe I went back to upstate New York. Or maybe I worked at a bookstore in DC's Dupont Circle for a few years. I could have even deejayed reggae on the radio at Tenley Circle, or perhaps I started a fish company with my brother. Muddled minds might mistake memories momentarily. Maybe.

Anyway, for these next few years, during which I worked a number of odd jobs, Jamaica was still on my mind. This was the impetus for me working—so I could go there again. And again and again. One time I went with a girlfriend to Kingston, and even though many people had warned me to stay away from the place, I fell in love with it. The energy. The music. The realness of Jamaica—and not where the tourists came. Everyday life being lived by everyday people. I got to know Kingston well, but Portland Parish and Port Antonio was still the place for me. The tranquil, lush side of the island which was not inundated with tourists. And as I had established roots in Hope Bay, I often found myself back in Port Antonio. I loved it there.

I remember one time driving over the mountain from Hope Bay to Kingston on the small road through Annotto Bay. I had about a pound of weed in the trunk and Dreadie was driving with me, and of course the cops stopped us at a roadblock and searched the car. Whenever a dread and tourist were moving together the police thought something was up. I took the rap for the weed since it was mine, and when I offered to pay the head cop for the offense I was shocked that he would have no part of that. I had never seen a cop in Jamaica NOT take money for finding ganja on someone. This was not making sense to me. Corruption was rampant on the island, and with their meager salaries cops would almost always supplement their income with a little pocket money when they got the opportunity. No one in Jamaica really cared about ganja anyway. They told Dreadie to leave and ran me back down the mountain in a police jeep to Annotto Bay and gave me a tour of the jail. It was pretty dismal. They then took me before a judge, as they like to try tourists right away if they are caught with ganja. The judge said I could pay a fine of ten dollars or spend thirty days in jail. I like to joke with people here (with a straight face, of course) that I refused to pay the ten bucks and spent the thirty days in jail. And it's unbelievable that people would even believe me.

By the time I started RAS Records many years later, I never missed an opportunity to travel to Jamaica. My passport was full of stamps. The customs guys at the airport would flip page after page and just stamp me again. Instead of going into Montego Bay and over to Negril I would fly into Kingston and then head to Port Antonio. I usually did some recording or business relating to my distribution company in Kingston, and then would chill out for a few days in Porty. I even worked out a deal with Air Jamaica where they put their logo on my album covers in exchange for free flights to Jamaica.

Life was good. Freddie McGregor and the Studio One Band played at my wedding. I spent my honeymoon in Jamaica and drove all over the island with my wife, enjoying everything the country had to offer. It was heavy mango season and I bought a dozen mangoes at the Port Antonio market. I offered one to my wife who said, "Maybe later." I explained to her that there wouldn't be any left later, that's how good they were.

Each day we would drive over to San San Beach; we went to Kingston; we drove and ate our way across the southern part of the island and ended up in Negril. On that trip I actually acquired three acres of land overlooking the Caribbean in a place called Canewood. It was on the way to a place known as Paradise. I have never done anything with that land but there are mango, pineapple, soursop, pimento, coconuts, and lots of other great fruits growing there.

Kingston became where I worked and Port Antonio became the place I relaxed. I rarely even ventured near Negril or the touristy parts of the island anymore. I think I may have started to become a Jamaican. Heartically. My wife and I were planning to go back to Port Antonio for our first anniversary and decided to inquire about renting a villa near San San Beach where we had spent most of our honeymoon. The villa was called San Cove, and it was right on the water directly across from Monkey Island. The owner told me that they were thinking of selling it to a hotel. I immediately said I would like to buy it. My wife looked at me like I was crazy. I made arrangements to send the owner Joe, who lived in New York, a check for $10,000 that same day to let him know I was serious. Sometimes my impulsiveness has gotten me into trouble, but sometimes it has helped me deal quickly with the situation at hand.

The house was amazing. Overlooking a beautiful piece of the water with a coral reef about a hundred yards out that would break all the waves and leave a shimmering mirrored pool right in front of our house. And Monkey Island, which you could swim or boat out to, was uninhabited and had a beautiful little beach with coconut palms and other tropical foliage. The real beauty of this precious little island was that it broke up the view of the expansive horizon with its greenness and rocks. It was heaven on earth and still to this day is one of the most beautiful spots I have ever been to on this planet of ours.

So we ended up buying the house, even though we were never quite sure where the money would come from to pay off the mortgage—we knew we wanted to own it free and clear as soon as we could. We had a permanent staff of a cook, housekeeper, and maid. We made up a brochure to rent the place and this income helped cover our expenses. People would pay in advance, so we could use that money toward the mortgage, the upkeep of the house, and the salaries of our staff. Staff was paid every week regardless of whether there were guests staying there or not. And because we might be paid six months in advance to confirm a booking, we ended up having the cash flow to pay Joe and the co-owner Richie each month as well. In fact, we all became good friends and would play practical jokes on each other. And I'd have a constant stream of guests at the house, who I always let stay for free so they could experience the real beauty of Jamaica. *Mi casa es tu casa*.

One time Joe and his wife Skippy came down for Thanksgiving with some friends of theirs. My family had been there about a month before, and I devised a sinister plan to really mess with them. Typically we would rent the house from Saturday to Saturday. But since it was Thanksgiving they were coming in on a Thursday. I had arranged for the manager of Mystic Revealers, Julius Chin Yee, to be at the house on that Thursday with a bunch of people. Julius could be pretty threatening, and I wanted him to play the part to the fullest. He would tell them that he had rented the house through Saturday. I also got the staff and even my local rental agent in Jamaica in on the plan. Joe and Skippy and their friends arrived after a twelve-hour trip from New York to find the house occupied by a bunch of Jamaicans with towels all over and people hanging out on our dock. The staff told them they were not expected till Saturday. And Julius told them in no uncertain terms that Doctor Dread had rented them the house till then. Can you imagine how they were feeling? Joe went to speak with the rental agent down the road to inquire how this mix-up could have transpired—but the agent could not hold back her laughter. They returned to the house with Joe, and the cat was now out of the bag. The whole town thought it was very funny, and we still laugh about this now.

Jamaica became our real home. Our staff became like family and Yvette, the cook, was there with us for fourteen years, as was Rose the housekeeper. Both our kids became comfortable in Jamaica and they still have an intense love for the island and its people. My wife's parents would come down there, and I even got my own parents to visit. I would have many of the RAS artists come and enjoy the house as well; it was only right that I could share with them what the fruits of their labor had afforded me. I loved to swim in the area in front of our house with this big white-spotted stingray. Flabba Holt would always joke with me about how I loved to swim with that "rip ray." The Jamaicans were surprised to see me jump into the water when it came by the house, but I loved its graceful manner when it moved its wings gently up and down as it glided through the sea. The fishermen would come right up to our dock and sell us fish and lobsters, and our staff would prepare amazing Jamaican meals for us and all our friends. A nice fresh fruit punch with rum in the afternoon—and waking from your nap in time for dinner was always the perfect end to a perfect day. We truly felt blessed and wanted to share this place with as many people as we could. Portland Parish, which many Jamaicans will tell you is the most beautiful part of the island, was so laid back. Waterfalls, mountains, remote beaches . . . and the best jerk chicken in the world came from Boston Beach, which was five miles down the road. It was there that I learned the real secrets of making the best possible jerk, a food that is now common all over the world.

I cannot count the number of times my family came to stay in Port Antonio. One of my most cherished memories is going to the house on my fiftieth birthday and watching my two sons snorkeling together as I looked out over the water from the upper balcony. Believe me, that moment brought tears to my eyes. This never would have happened without Jah's blessing, and I must give thanks itinually for all the gifts He has bestowed upon I and I. Jamaica is just so much of part of who I am that I feel more natural and comfortable when I am there than in the United States. Jamaica, land I love.

FATIS

Walking down the road with a pistol in your waist,
Johnny you're too bad . . .
—The Slickers, from *The Harder They Come* sound track

"**G**ary, I need your help right away. I am stuck in jail in Baltimore and I need a lawyer. Please, right away." It was not the first time I had accepted a collect call from a prison with one of my artists asking for bail money, but this was different.

Only two Jamaicans in the reggae business ever referred to me as Gary: one was saxophone legend Dean Fraser, and the next was one of my best friends, Philip "Fatis" Burrell. From when I first met Fatis at a party in Miami for *Reggae Report* magazine, he and I had formed a special bond. He had just started producing reggae music and had a Yellowman album he had completed. He told me he did not really know anyone in the business but felt he could trust me, so he wanted to make a commitment to work with RAS as his label for the rest of the world outside the Caribbean. There was something

I instantly liked about Fatis. He was a serious thinker but when he loosened up he would joke and laugh about how peculiar he found life and people to be. He also read his Bible religiously, and Rastafari was of paramount importance in his life and grew to become more evident in the artists he signed and promoted.

Over time I came to find out that Fatis had been a bodyguard for Michael Manley, the former prime minister of Jamaica, and was seriously involved with the PNP political party. Now, when it comes to politics in Jamaica, dem nah joke. You pick a side and do whatever is required to help maintain power for that side. I remember having lunch one day at Minnie's vegetarian restaurant in Kingston, and Bunny Rugs from Third World asked me what party I supported. I tried to get out of it by saying I was an American and really had no affiliation with either party, and he told me that my answer was unacceptable. That in Jamaica you cannot have your car in neutral, you must put it into gear. And just like my faith in Rastafari, I also kept my political views of Jamaica to myself. But my close affiliations with Fatis and others may have led some to believe I was a PNP supporter.

It is all politricks anyway. Promises that never get fulfilled. Election time in Jamaica would get violent with many shootings perpetrated in the ghettos where the PNP and JLP staged turf wars. The higher-ranking politicos would supply guns to the impoverished youth there, and have them carry out acts of bloodshed to disrupt the country and keep the people on edge. This political violence from the '70s and '80s has since calmed down a bit, and elections are now held in a more civilized environment. But back then it was some serious shit.

In order to get away from the bad-man business before it took them out, many dons of the ghetto turned to music. And when you look at the hip-hop world you see people like Jay-Z, 50 Cent, P Diddy, and countless others who have been able to transform their lives as dealers, hustlers, and badasses to become successful music executives and recording artists. Bunny Wailer even laid out the theory that this was intentionally done by music executives to calm down the violence. To make way for these tough guys to find a more lucrative lifestyle in the music industry. I am not sure how true that is, but it is interesting to consider.

In Jamaica it was especially true that many ghetto youths sought to hit it big in the music business to lift them from the poverty that seemed to keep them entrenched in the quagmire of ghetto suffering. They even called themselves "sufferers." And many, including myself, believe that some of the greatest reggae music ever was born from this sufferer's spirit. (You can say the same about the blues, which has similar origins.)

So Fatis left the bad-man business behind and became a music producer. He started a label known as Xterminator, an interesting name with a not-so-subtle innuendo. I believe he may have run some minibus routes around Kingston which also had vehicles named *Xterminator*. You didn't mess with Fatis. I guess he got that name because he was well over six feet tall and heavyset. A devout Rasta, he did not trim his hair or beard, and did not eat pork, chicken, or meat. Only fish. Not even shellfish. For Rastas, like the Jews, only fish with scales are to be consumed.

Whenever I would come to Jamaica, Fatis would

be the first to arrive at my hotel. Riding up on his motorcycle and always bringing me a good draw of weed. Many hotels had a rule against having Jamaicans come to your room, and you were instructed to meet them in the lobby. You know, wouldn't want the Jamaican riffraff disturbing the guests. I threw this rule out the window and on some occasions the hotels preferred to have me find other accommodations—I never have been too good at following rules. My choice hotel in Kingston became the Terra Nova. This was a large property that was formerly owned by the Blackwell family, and was where little Chris Blackwell had grown up. It was outside of New Kingston and had only two floors, a nice pool, and a large patio for breakfast. I never liked the high-rise hotels in New Kingston that tried to be pretentious like Miami. Places like the Pegasus and Hilton where most foreign businessmen would stay. I wanted the real Jamaican vibe.

The Terra Nova knew me as Doctor Dread, and during my waking hours when I was not working in the studio there was always a steady stream of artists, producers, and the like coming through to discuss business and other matters. I loved to hold court on the terrace there with those great breakfasts and treat my guests to a nice healthy Jamaican meal. You know: ackee, callaloo, dumplings. Jamaican stylee. To let them enjoy some of the first-class service and food of this fine establishment. I have always believed that the poor should be able to experience the fine things in life, that these should not just be reserved for the rich.

Fatis was a natural when it came to discovering new talent and taking the steps to create the right career moves for his artists. I am not sure if he was always directing the musicians and artists in the studio, but like Coxsone Dodd of Studio One before him, he cultivated an environment where the musicians had the freedom to really create. Many Jamaican producers like Junjo Lawes, Linval Thompson, and Bunny Lee played the role of an "executive producer." They would set things up in the studio and then be out on the street hustling to pay for all the expenses. Fatis worked with Luciano, Sizzla, Capleton, and Sanchez, to name just a few, and RAS had the honor of putting out some of their first releases. These artists stuck close to Fatis and he was their boss. It wasn't about money; it was about brethren working together and sharing what came in. And Fatis was with them every step of the way, and people knew not to fuck with him or his artists.

You did not want to make Fatis vex. I heard stories about how he had beat someone up pretty bad for messing with something he should not have been messing with. How he had been in jail on a murder charge, and then the charges were dropped. He told me how he had been in England and saw his own picture on the front page of the *Daily Mirror*, and it said that he was a Jamaican hit man who was in the UK to assassinate Margaret Thatcher. Margaret fucking Thatcher! He swore there was no truth to this but he still made sure to leave England as quickly as possible. When I visited him after he got a nice town house in the uptown area of Kingston, the first thing he did was pull out his gun from his closet to show me. Like he wanted to impress me.

I am not totally sure why but many Jamaicans thought I was a tough guy and a gunman, but truth be told I have never owned a gun. I may have perpetuated this rumor early in my reggae career when I was on tour with Freddie McGregor and the Studio One Band. Some Jamaicans always act like badasses. I knew if I was gonna last in the reggae business I needed a strong backbone to stand up to their aggressive posturing. I would say, "You Jamaicans think you are bad but I am a direct descendent of the Corleone family and we take people out like *this*." I would pull my hand across my neck and nod my head slightly. I knew many Jamaicans had seen all the *Godfather* movies. I was always good at saying things with a straight face and having people believe me. When I saw how they reacted and backed off, I just let it ride, and I heard it got spread around Jamaica that Doctor Dread was a badass and not to be fucked with. A Corleone. Shit, I'm not even Italian!

I even remember at my fish job after my career in the music business evaporated that one of my coworkers came up to me and we were arguing about some incident; he was standing over me trying to be threatening. I told him: "Back off or I am gonna fuck you up." I was not sure what that meant, and it really was a pretty open-ended statement, but it seemed to do the trick. So I added that one to my repertoire and use it whenever I need to. This same person at work later said to me that our coworkers never believed I had ever actually killed anyone myself, but did believe I had paid to have people killed. Of course I would not deny this, as I wanted them to believe I was a badass, though it still puzzles me to this day when I remember how so many people thought Doctor Dread was a gangster.

So Fatis had his own reputation even if I never saw

it. We would laugh and joke around and hang out like good friends do. I knew he had been close to Tony Welch back in the day. Tony had licensed me an Eek-A-Mouse album and had mentioned that he and Fatis knew each other. They had not seen each other for many years and one time Tony was driving up from Florida while Fatis and I were working in the studio in Washington, DC. I told Tony to come by and see us. I always like getting people together in these types of situations—and it was great seeing these old friends stay up all night talking about old times. In the recent Bob Marley documentary that Ziggy Marley and Chris Blackwell put together, Tony is interviewed and is labeled as a PNP enforcer. I had to laugh when I saw that come up on the screen.

One day the FBI showed up at my office wanting to know why there were checks from RAS Records to Tony Welch. They also said they were aware of my past involvement with the sale of large amounts of high-grade sinsemilla. I asked if Tony was in some kind of trouble. They told me he had been found with $500,000 in cash, and they later stopped a tractor trailer filled with Mexican weed on its way from Texas to New York; they said it was Tony's weed and he had been moving tractor trailers on a regular basis. I have to admit I was kind of surprised to hear this. Tony and I had only done a very small deal on an Eek-A-Mouse record, and when he had offered to lend RAS money the night he and Fatis and I were hanging out in the studio, I told him I was okay, but thanks for the offer. In retrospect, even though I was always hard up for cash, I am glad I declined.

I explained to the feds that my weed-selling days were long finished, and that I was making more as a music executive than any of them were making. I showed them the CD of Eek-A-Mouse with Tony's name on it, and even produced royalty statements displaying the sums owed to him with check numbers on the page. They handed me the complete indictment of Tony to read, and I felt very bad for him. The good thing is that I really knew nothing about what he was involved with. He ended up doing around seven years in the pen in Florida, and then got deported back to Jamaica. He still calls me asking how he can make money from his recordings, but I have had to tell him that these days the music business is not the same.

I remember once sitting around in a hotel room in Jamaica with Fatis and Tony Welch discussing a business deal. Sly Dunbar also showed up, and after Fatis and Tony left I was sitting there with Sly and he said to me, "Doctor Dread, do you realize who you just had together here in your room? If certain people knew who was here they would probably come in here and arrest you all!" I just laughed. Tony was like a big teddy bear and Fatis and I were family. I sometimes wonder if bad men stop being so rough and tough once you've been accepted by them; with Tony and Fatis, it was more like a bunch of friends joking together and having a good time. It reminds me of the song "Welcome to Jamrock," when Damian Marley sings, *"When bad man stop laugh and block off traffic."* In my twisted mind, I always hear it as, *"When bad man start laugh and block off traffic."*

Fatis always loved to visit us at our house in Port Antonio. I had grown close to his entire family. His wife Donna. His oldest son Kareem and my oldest son Eric were the same age. His daughter Nefertiti. As I have said, I loved it when different artists and Jamaican friends would come and hang out there. Fatis. My good friend Buffy. Bunny Wailer. Burning Spear. Some of them had never known this part of the island. I know it was I who turned Fatis on to this area, and he loved to come to Frenchman's Cove (my favorite beach in the world) and hang out in the river there to get away from the hustle and bustle of Kingston. Fatis and his family were always welcome. Once, Fatis unexpectedly showed up at our place with an entourage of thirteen people. We went into panic mode: How would we feed everyone? Where would they sleep? We couldn't entertain all these guests, since we were about to head back to the States and had pretty much wiped out our food and supplies. This became known as the Fatis Incident, which was almost an international debacle—but fortunately he and his crew ended up finding a hotel up on the hill and everything turned out to be irie and nice.

One of the best stories Fatis told me is when he was pulled over and the police officer asked him, "Do you have any marijuana in the car?" Now remember that Fatis was an intimidating man who was both respected and feared in certain circles in Jamaica. All Fatis could do was laugh. He told the officer, "Listen. If you ever pull over anyone from the Xterminator Crew and they DO NOT have ganja in their possession, you should immediately take them to the station and book them for NOT having ganja." What could the officer do but laugh? Was he really going to search Fatis and look for weed? The same Fatis who would fire up a spliff while in the presence of the prime minister of Jamaica? There were no pretenses with Fatis.

* * *

Another Fatis incident that got a little out of control was when Sinéad O'Connor traveled to Jamaica to record a reggae CD. As many of us older folks can recall, Sinéad had sung the Bob Marley song "War" on *Saturday Night Live*, and at its culmination tore up a photograph of the pope. All on one of the most-watched TV shows on national television. This did not go over so well and really mashed up what had once been a successful career for Sinéad. She had been selling millions of records and her voice was regarded as one of the best. And although she disappeared from the scene for a while, she would occasionally resurface and release some music.

In any case, she had gotten deep into the reggae and the Rasta thing and wanted to go to Jamaica for the first time and record an album there. At this point RAS Records was owned by Sanctuary Records Group and her manager was working there, and someone from Sanctuary put the two of us together so I could help arrange the logistics of her trip. I set up the hotel. Arranged for my good brethren Buffy to pick her up at the airport and stick with her and make sure she was okay. I even connected her up with Burning Spear in New York. Sinéad and I actually got on quite well and I had no reason to do anything other than help her accomplish her goal of navigating through the runnings of Jamaica to make a great reggae record.

I have always felt that regardless of who makes reggae more popular, it will help the entire genre and there will be some trickle-down lifting the many people involved in keeping the music alive. So I opened up my world of Jamaica and reggae to Sinéad, and did my best to make sure things went well. I knew that once she was in Buffy's hands, all would be good. She also wanted to meet Sizzla, who at the time was the most militant and hottest firebrand in the business and was managed by Fatis. And although it seemed that everything was going well, several months after her trip was completed I came home to find a disconcerting phone message she had left on our answering machine at home.

It follows in full: "Gary, it's Sinéad O'Connor. I am calling on the seventeenth of February. I am going to follow this call with an e-mail that concerns something a little birdie told me about something that apparently—allegedly—you and Fatis had cooked up concerning my manager a year ago when I was in Jamaica. So I'll be following up this call with an e-mail, but I just want you both to know I have heard of this alleged plan you have cooked up. I don't expect to get an honest answer from either of you, but I'm warning you, as an Irish person, that although you all may think you're very tough there in Jamaica, we're a lot fucking tougher over here—and if any of you so much as laid a hand on anybody that I know, believe me, you'd both be very sorry. And I don't really give a shit, to be honest, so I want you to know that I know this plan you had regarding my manager. And I want you to know, Gary, that if you set foot ever at one of my shows I will have you arrested. Never come to one of my shows. Never come backstage at one of my shows. Never come front stage at one of my shows. Do not step into a Sinéad O'Connor show unless you want to end up in jail. Okay? And don't fuck with me, and tell big fat Fatis not to fuck with me either, because you don't want the fucking IRA getting on you. And believe me, they will. You all might think you're tough but you don't want to fuck with an Irish woman and you don't want to fuck with the fucking IRA. If I see you at one of my shows, you're fucked. So don't bother your arse."

Well, I guess I could make something up really cool at this point abut how the IRA burned down my house or how Sinéad O'Connor punched me in the nose and it was all bloody as the police led me off to jail, but this book is titled *The Half That's Never Been Told*, which means there is still another half I have not told you about, and which I have no plans of doing.

Let's just say that she finally apologized, and now I have to chuckle when I think about this whole incident. Sinéad ended up canceling her tour plans with Ziggy and Stephen Marley, and I was called to have Bunny Wailer fill in for her. It was a beautiful tour and I guess Jah does work in some mysterious ways, so when one door closes another will open. The last I heard of Sinéad is that she was on *Oprah* talking about her bipolar condition. It must have kicked in that day she decided to leave the phone message.

Back to Fatis and that desperate call I got from him in jail. He did not sound good at all, and I needed to respond quickly. After visiting him in jail and getting a brief synopsis of his situation, I quickly hooked him up with a lawyer from Maryland, and Fatis also informed me that he was having Dudley Thompson come up from Jamaica to oversee his situation. I had never met Dudley before, but he had served as ambassador to Nigeria and held other high-ranking political positions in Jamaica. By the time I encountered him he was well over seventy, but was a compelling figure with a keen insight into life, due to his extraordinary experiences. He told me about representing Jomo Kenyatta when he was being tried by the Kenyan government for creating a civil disturbance in his attempt to free Kenya from British colonial rule. (Kenyatta is considered the father of that country and is credited with gaining its liberation, hence the name *Kenya*.) Interestingly, while staging guerilla warfare on the occupying forces in their country, Kenyatta and his Mau Mau warriors wore dreadlocks. Dudley also explained he was glad that this was one of the few times he actually lost a case, since Kenyatta was ironically safer behind bars than out in the open—if he was out on the streets the government would have done everything it could to kill him, but it would have had a harder time explaining his death in custody.

In any case, Fatis had evidently gotten busted carrying around $100,000 in cash back to Jamaica. It was stashed on his body and he was apprehended while boarding an Air Jamaica flight from Baltimore. The money had been linked back to a robbery where a drug deal turned into a rip-off, and someone had gotten killed. Fatis had no involvement in this whole robbery but had been asked by a family member to assist in carrying the money to Jamaica. If you carry over $10,000 in cash out of the US, you are supposed to declare it and make a statement about where you obtained it. Fatis had neglected to do this and he got busted.

Dudley worked with his lawyers to formulate a defense, and after seventeen days they had worked out an arrangement with the police that Fatis would forfeit the money and could finally return to Jamaica.

When I picked him up at the jail he was extremely weak and I brought him back to my house so he could gradually regain his strength. He had been through hell. He had not eaten in seventeen days, and was dangerously dehydrated. I made a simple potato broth soup to gradually reintroduce food to his system. Sipping the soup with him on my front porch, I could tell he was tired. Extremely tired. In the middle of the night he stumbled to the bathroom and was throwing up and collapsed on the floor and could not get up. I reasoned with him to go to the hospital but he was very stubborn. He told me that he just needed to rest and that he would be all right. I told him that there was no fucking way he was *not* going to the hospital and to stop arguing with me or he would be sorry.

I finally got him to the emergency room, and after receiving these intravenous drips all night he was a completely different person in the morning. He was like Fatis again, and he told me he was really fucking hungry, so we feasted at Legal Sea Foods and he ate like a man who had not had any food in weeks! We both knew that I had saved his life that night, but we didn't need to speak about it. They say that sometimes words are better left unspoken. But the bond which had already existed between us was further strengthened. I was scared as shit that night when he collapsed on the bathroom floor, and I give thanks to Jah he did not leave me then, as I am gripped with a kind of loneliness when people I really care about move on to the other side.

The last time I saw Fatis was in 2010 for Gregory Isaacs's funeral. As I've mentioned, there was a big tribute concert for Gregory at the Ranny Williams Center in Kingston and most of the major reggae stars were there that night to pay tribute to the Cool Ruler. I let Fatis know I would be traveling in for this and he actually came out to the show. He never really went out in public and especially not to a concert; he kept very much to himself and his closest brethren. When I saw him that night he told me, "It was only a man like you who could get me to leave my yard."

The next day was Gregory's funeral so Fatis and I met the following morning at my hotel for breakfast. As usual, we sat out under the mango trees and had a splendid breakfast of callaloo, dumplings, yam, and ackee with saltfish.

Fatis explained to me that I was now an "untouchable" in Jamaica. I liked the way that sounded but I needed some explanation. He told me that because of all I had done for Jamaica and the people there, no one could lay a hand on me. Even if someone had a beef with me, they had to lay off. Coming from Fatis, that felt pretty good. *An untouchable.* I liked that.

Fatis's breakup with his wife Donna impacted him in a big way. He lost his home, his recording tapes, and it hit him to the core in a way that only a life partner can mash up a man of strength. I had become close to his eldest son Kareem, who was an exact match of his father, not just in looks but also with the same vibes and mannerisms. We discussed how I might be able to help Kareem put out some of Fatis's unreleased music, so he could generate some much-needed money for the family. I bought Kareem a plane ticket to DC and set him up in the studio with a suitcase full of DAT tapes he had brought from Jamaica, and hooked him up with a new computer and all the necessary software. Unfortunately, when he got back to Jamaica, everything we bought Kareem, including the original DATs, was burned up in a fire. It's like everything went from bad to worse. We got Kareem the material he needed to help himself, but it all got taken from him, and I just didn't have the money to put him back in business again.

During this time in Kingston, after his relationship had fallen apart, Fatis did not look good and I could see that he was consumed by stress. Mashed up. It was late 2011, around the time Beres Hammond made a tour stop in Baltimore. I showed up that night with a check for $75,000 from SoundExchange, where I had been on the board of directors, since Beres had unwittingly been accruing royalties for years. He was happy to see me—and it wasn't about the money either. We were always cool and had good talks about music and the business, and I brought up Fatis. Beres was tight with him, since Fatis had produced many of his biggest tunes. I called up Fatis in Jamaica on my cell phone and put them on the line together. They had a good talk, and I told Fatis I would be in touch. That I would not forget about him. And I also asked Beres to keep in touch with him.

Within two weeks, Fatis had a serious stroke. He was in the hospital, and from what I could gather from others, he was in pretty bad shape. He was only fifty-seven years young. All I could do was to pray that he would come through this and be able to get on with his life—but he never made it.

He had passed on to the other side and I was deeply

saddened. It really hit me hard. I miss him and I miss calling him on his birthday, July 23, the same day His Imperial Majesty Emperor Haile Selassie I was born. I never missed calling him on that day to wish him a happy birthday. He and Joseph Hill from Culture are the two people I most look forward to hanging out with when I myself move on into the hereafter. Even more than my own father. Fatis, I love you. Jah bless and protect you in peace. Gary.

SOUTH AMERICA

Yo soy un hombre sincero
De donde crece la palma,
Y antes de morirme quiero
Echar mis versos del alma . . .

I am a sincere man from where the palm tree grows,
And before I die I want to share these verses of my soul . . .

—José Martí, from "Guantanamera"

When I showed up for my final day of high school in 1972 I had thirty joints rolled up in my pocket. I had seen a Western movie about this one-armed cowboy named Lefty who could roll a perfect cigarette with only one hand, and I was so impressed I became an expert joint roller. I lit each joint, took a hit, and then passed it to the other students on the quad. There was a huge cloud of marijuana smoke over Bethesda, Maryland, that day. Twenty years later my wife's cousin, who was a hair stylist in Virginia, mentioned to a customer that Deb had married Gary Himelfarb (a.k.a. Doctor Dread). Her client said she had gone to high school with me and told her this same story about how I had the whole quad immersed in a huge cloud of marijuana smoke. I guess this is how urban legends get started. I did not care much about the possible repercussions as I was going off to South America in a few days.

Most of my fellow students were going to college to become doctors or lawyers, but I had worked my final year of high school at a piss lab in downtown DC and had saved up a good amount of money. The lab was pretty disgusting. We would test the piss of soldiers and heroin addicts to see if they were using drugs. It was the worst job I ever had. I would pour urine samples into test tubes that had a reactive chemical agent which could then be analyzed to see if there were drugs in the urine. I always came to work wasted and would pour red wine into grape soda bottles so I could drink during my shift to put up with the environment. I also used to drive around to methadone clinics across the city and pick up urine samples in this big old station wagon. I saw firsthand how down-and-out these junkies looked—and although I have tried almost every drug known to man, I never, ever stuck a needle in my arm. I was so turned off by the predicament of these junkies that it kept me from going too far down that road. No thanks.

I was only seventeen but I was ready to go out and experience the real world and get away from what I considered to be a suburb filled with Naugahyde chairs and people whose whole lives were dedicated to making money and raising families. (In retrospect, I admit that there is nothing wrong with this, and maybe that is what the American dream is all about.) I was running away. A friend named Tom Quinn was stationed in Bogotá as a foreign correspondent for the *Washington Post*. He had sent numerous letters to my friend Charlie Becker and told him that we could come visit him and stay on his farm in Popayán, Colombia. It seemed like an exciting adventure, so I boarded a plane by myself and flew into Barranquilla on the north coast. Little did I know that this would sow a seed of wanderlust in me that took root and has stayed with me my entire life. My awe at meeting people of all different cultures and social backgrounds would become a reason for my very existence. This way of becoming worldly is something I have tried to pass on to my family.

On this first trip to Colombia, I stayed at a small hotel in Santa Marta and hung around with a bunch of Colombians my age, picking up Spanish very quickly. I had a girlfriend Nora there, and it's easier to learn another language if you have a partner to help teach you. After two weeks I began to dream in Spanish and that is when I knew my transition from American to Latino was really coming on. Nora and I visited her parents in Bucaramanga but I was a scruffy hippie and was never welcomed into her family. After going back to Santa Marta I had the harebrained idea that I could sell weed to tourists who frequented the outdoor cafés along the coast there. I would put it in little airmail envelopes and carry them in my muchilla. I talked to a Colombian about buying some, and the next thing I knew there were two police officers in their green uniforms standing over me.

They led me off to the police station and looked in my bag and found all these envelopes of marijuana. What the fuck was I thinking? I was thrown in jail, and I can tell you that Colombian jails are no four-star accommodation. Drifting asleep in my cell I would be awakened by rats that would come from out of the walls, and I had to stomp on the floor to chase them away. Maybe this is why I became such a light sleeper. It was an extremely unpleasant experience, as there is nothing worse (nothing!) than losing your freedom. It was not an easy week for me but I got through it and was soon set free.

My next trip to Colombia came about six months later. My friend Tui and I drove in my Volvo P1800 sports car to stay with my aunt and uncle in Florida so we could fly the cheapest way to Barranquilla on Avianca Airlines. My parents had bought me this car for my seventeenth birthday and I loved driving it. They handed me the keys and said it was mine and I think I was the happiest kid on the planet. I learned how to drive a stick shift on this little sports car and I believe this is when my love affair with cool automobiles first germinated inside me.

Tui was a big blues fan and had turned me on to the blues in high school. Lots of blues. He was also the first person who ever played reggae music for me. It was 1972, and I had just returned from that first trip to South America. He played Bob Marley and the sound track to *The Harder They Come*. I was completely blown away. Having soaked up the tropics and experienced a new culture made me ripe for this island beat. And the powerful message of Bob Marley spoke to my political and spiritual sensibilities. Tui likes to laugh and say that he created a monster. I was already known as "The Doctor" at the time, and this is where the embryonic "Doctor Dread" first came into being. I can never forget sitting in his house on MacArthur Boulevard in Washington, DC, and hearing those records.

In Colombia, Tui and I rented a house outside of Santa Marta with some other travelers we met. We were up in the mountains, and houses would go for around five or ten dollars a month. We would string up hammocks to sleep in, smoke lots of dope, and find food each day in the markets. It was a mellow existence and the time passed slowly. There were jugo stands in the Santa Marta market where we would get all kinds of incredible fruit smoothies. A vendor there once circled our truck and shouted out, "Chicharones, chicharones!" I loved the way that word sounded, so I decided to buy whatever it was he was selling. When I opened the wrapper, I discovered pig skin with these repulsive little hairs sticking out. I was a vegetarian, so I gave them away to someone else on the truck, but I still laugh whenever I see people eating pork rinds. *Chi-cha-ron-es!!!*

One day we went to this river that had twenty-five-year-old mango trees all around it. It was a rocky river with many pools cascading down a beautiful tropical mountain. All these Colombian kids were jumping into the water and eating mangoes. We would sit in the trees and eat the mangoes, then cool off in the pools of water. Once, we gathered up more than 250 mangoes into burlap bags and brought them back to our place, which is an image that will remain in my mind forever. And I asked myself then why this was not as good as being in an American suburb with its homogeneous society with picket fences and tacky little boxes. These Colombian kids all had big smiles on their faces and the surroundings were magical.

After hanging around the north coast for a while we eventually made our way down to Medellin and Cali. We traveled by bus, and there was wild cumbia music blasting the entire trip, which—along with the live chickens and goats onboard and the constant threat of someone ripping off our backpacks—made it difficult to sleep. Our plan was to score some weed in Cali and then head on to San Agustín. The pre-Colombian Indians had built a number of stone idols all around San Agustín, so the place was considered sacred. It was also known as an area where people were taking psilocybin mushrooms and many American and European hippies had made their way there to experiment with these mind-altering hallucinogenics.

One afternoon, we were sitting in a park in Cali when we were approached by two Colombians who looked like hippies. (Of course I had on my colorful Ecuadorian poncho.) The four of us went back to our hotel room and Tui and I expressed our desire to buy a pound of weed—and that we wanted the very best. It was decided that I would go with the one guy and Tui would remain back in the room with his friend.

We headed into some ghetto neighborhood and into a house and found this rough-looking guy and his wife. She was cooking and he had some different types of weed for me to try. I sampled the first one and said, "No, I need better." The second one did not pass the test either. I took one hit of the third one and immediately said, "Yes, this is the one." He told me to give him the money and he would go and get the weed for me. I refused. He said that is how it works and I explained that I could not trust him. He said it could not happen any other way, so I gave him the money but told him if he did not return that I would do something crazy like kill his wife.

I peered out a little crack in the door and watched him talking to one of those green-uniform cops on the street. I was sure I was being set up. I had already spent time in a Colombian jail and had no intention of returning. Typical story: Gringo gives dealer money for weed. Dealer gives weed to gringo and has cops waiting to bust him. Dealer and cops split the money, dealer gets his weed back, and gringo goes to jail.

I was nervous as hell. The guy from the park who was in the house with me assured me everything was okay. Soon the dealer came back with the brick of weed. I quickly examined it and put it in the back of my pants, covered up by my poncho. The two of us then left the house and caught a taxi to the hotel. Tui and the other Colombian dude were sitting there waiting for us. When I took out the weed and we started to roll it up, the Colombians exclaimed, "Ay, carajo, es la sinsemilla!"

The small green buds had red hairs, and amazingly there were no seeds. *Sinsemilla* is a Spanish word meaning *without seeds*. It was 1973, and I will challenge anyone to say they knew about sinsemilla this early. That first hit was nice, but I never expected something this monumental. The rest is history.

You may wonder why I speak so openly about marijuana. Weed. Ganja. Kushumpeng. It has many names and also many uses. This is a plant that Jah put onto this earth. And I cannot overstand how a plant can be made illegal. Weed never killed anybody. If you smoke too much you will most likely just fall asleep. You cannot OD on it. Alcohol makes some people mean and get into fights. Marijuana makes you mellow and not want to fight. So many deaths each year are caused by drunk drivers, but I do not believe there are statistics which confirm deaths from the use of marijuana in car accidents. Drunk people go into violent rages and hit their wives or kids. Marijuana does not do that to you. In a city like Amsterdam where weed is essentially legal, people are not lighting up all over the place. People are not trying to get kids "hooked" on marijuana. No one is pushing it on you in some alley or dark corner of a park. It is all very civilized. The people who choose to smoke do so respectfully and those who do not care to smoke go about their lives. No big deal.

The same can be said for the coca plant. Many Indians in South America use the coca leaf to combat the ill-effects of high altitude. And they use it for endurance for the longs walks to and from their villages. Jah also put the coca plant here on this earth.

But cocaine is different. Cocaine is made by man. And it is addictive and makes people do crazy things and ruins lots of people's lives. So I do differentiate between what is a natural plant and what is a drug. And even though I do not use marijuana anymore (the main reason being that when I do smoke, my brain starts going a million miles an hour and is filled with a preponderance of thoughts I cannot control until I begin to mellow into my high about an hour later), I still cannot believe this is considered an illegal drug. It is almost legal in many states, and I am sure it could provide much-needed revenues for our suffering economy. The healing of the nation. But time is the master and time will tell us what will be. For I and I marijuana is just a simple plant whose benefits have been overlooked by mainstream society.

So Tui and I continued on our way to San Agustín. It was an extremely long bus ride deep into the mountains. There was a hotel in town where all the foreigners stayed and where we found our friend Charlie Becker from high school, who had first told us about the marvels of Colombia. The three of us decided to rent a house, where we ate lots of fried plantains and did lots of mushrooms and explored the culture of the pre-Colombian people.

After a while, Tui and I ended up going back to Bogotá to experience some of what the capital had to offer. We found a steam room that used eucalyptus to open up your pores and we bought some cocaine and snorted it and went inside. I am not sure if we thought this up ourselves or had been told to try it. But just like Vicks VapoRub (which is made from eucalyptus) opens you up when you are congested, the eucalyptus opened up the nasal passages and the steam carried the effects of cocaine to the brain. It really was "cocaine, all around my brain."

We then flew back home to Miami. The Volvo P1800 was waiting there and we made the trip back up I-95 to DC.

At the time, my oldest brother Steve and his wife Judy were living in upstate New York. I had always looked up to Steve; of my three brothers, he and I were the closest and had the most similar lifestyle. He liked the hippie culture, though I was more of a militant and was reading Abbie Hoffman and Jerry Rubin and thinking about politics instead of just getting high. I remember my mom once found a copy of *Revolution for the Hell of It* and blamed it on Steve and he took the rap for me. My parents could never have imagined their sixteen-year-old would be reading such radical literature.

Steve had fallen into being a caretaker with a bunch of other people at a 440-acre estate in the Shawangunk Mountains. This was owned by an eccentric New Yorker named Thomas Ketchum who would sometimes come up and visit from the city. He went around pretending to be a priest, and I guess that was part of his persona, but he was wacky as a lunatic and he let all these hippies stay on his property almost rent-free. There was a massive Tudor mansion that had been a lodge, along with two smaller houses. The large house was occupied by the Intense Space Circus (a band that frequently played in Woodstock and would rehearse endlessly in the mansion) and the Theatre of Madness (a drama group who would do performances back in the city). The ice house was a small building occupied by my brother's best friend Steve Berman and his girlfriend Amy. My brother Steve and Judy were in another cottage over a garage.

I drove my Volvo P1800 up there and stayed with them. Some of us got menial jobs in the mountains but most of our time was spent hiking to the far cliffs, hanging out in the streams or in our teepee sauna, gardening, or tending to our goats. Steve and Judy really took good care of me and never put any pressure on me.

Soon a girl named Ava and her boyfriend Steve Cochran moved up to the area and rented a trailer not far from where we lived. I have always believed in the chemical attraction between people that it is fundamental to any deep relationship. And this attraction can turn sexual if that chemical reacts in the right way. It was obvious that Ava and I had that attraction, and before long Steve moved out and it was Ava and me in that trailer. Ava was my first true love. We were soul mates. She was from New York and somehow related to the actor Gene Tierney.

Eventually, Ava and I moved into the ice house where we lived the hippie lifestyle. We would lay in bed during the day and drink red wine and smoke weed and walk in the woods and talk about life and going to South America together. Ava was also a true nymphomaniac. That can be a good thing and it can also be a not-so-good thing. She said she lived to experience her next orgasm and that it was sex that she craved and wanted all the time. I was a novice but Ava taught me well. It did not matter where or when, it just mattered that we did it. She was a year younger than me but she had that New York City style and was so wild and free and I knew she could not be tamed. Freedom is a very precious commodity and allowing someone to be free and be themselves is one of the greatest gifts you can bestow. Allowing someone to just be who they are and not putting pressure on them to be something else. Accepting the good and bad we all have within ourselves.

Avacado and I were inseparable. We did everything together. We did acid and got high and really connected on a profound level. We once drove into New York and snuck into Madison Square Garden to see Bob Dylan and the Band perform. We were discovered hiding in a small closet in a dressing room but they let us stay anyway since we explained how we had come all the way from upstate and had no money. I remember Bob sitting at the piano that night and playing "Ballad of a Thin Man" and hallucinating as the stage moved up and down. I was not on drugs; it was just such an intense moment with those chords banging out from the piano that the whole place was moving around. The only other time that happened to me was at a Stevie Wonder show. That is the power of music.

I sold my Volvo P1800 for $1,700 and we got some more money together and booked our flights to Colombia. As usual we flew into Barranquilla, which was the closest city in Colombia to Miami. We spent time around the Santa Marta area and rented a house up in the mountains. Early on we made a trip high into the Sierra Nevada de Santa Marta, where the last of the true Arawak Indians lived. These people, the Kogi, are the same as the Carib Indians who were the original inhabitants of the Caribbean, including Jamaica, before Chris Columbus and subsequent Spanish explorers came and wiped them out. We encountered them as we hiked through these high mountains. They made their own clothes and chewed coca leaves. But the Kogi were not friendly and preferred to live away from the rest of society, so we did not really get the chance to know them.

Returning to our house in the mountains, we lived simply. It was a lesson in the basic task of feeding yourself each day so you can make it to tomorrow. It is amazing how many people on this planet live this way and never drive through a McDonald's to find their daily bread. But we were happy and in love. One time we took a trip up the coast from Santa Marta toward Venezuela. We were on a desolate beach where we decided to sleep our first night. The next day we were making love just out in the open on this isolated stretch of sand when I looked behind me and saw these young Colombian kids peering from behind some rocks with their thumbs up in the air, whistling with big smiles on their faces. I got up and chased them away but inside I was laughing. When we returned to our mountain house we realized we were covered with thousands of sand ticks. We got out the alcohol and scrubbed every inch of our bodies and finally killed them all off. Another adventure in paradise.

We spent about six weeks on the north coast. You could only get ninety-day visas when you entered Colombia so our plan was to stay in the country for three months and then head to Ecuador and get our visas renewed when we returned. We traveled by bus and settled into a small town near Cali. One day we went to the park there and encountered a man who offered to sell us a monkey, which we thought might make a nice addition to our country home. The monkey was asleep, but the man assured us it was just tired and not sick. We took the monkey back to our hotel room where it continued to rest all day. But then, late that night, the monkey started to attack us with its claws—it turned out to be a fierce, nocturnal jungle creature called an "oso arquero" (ant-eating bear). We were stuck with it in the hotel room all night and it was like being trapped in a horror film.

Another afternoon, we went to our neighbor's house

for a visit. In Colombia almost everyone has a pot of coffee on the stove at all times. I had brought my Spanish-English dictionary with me and was going through it with my elderly neighbor. I came across the word *judeo* (Jew) and asked what that meant to her. Her response was, "Those who killed God." These were her exact words. During our travels through the country, Ava and I had noticed that as the bus approached each small town, the largest and most obvious building was always the church. And teaching people that the Jews killed God was a fundamental part of their Catholic indoctrination.

Another time in Cali we went to receive a package at the main post office from Ava's mom in New York City. We were both strict vegetarians at the time and her mom had sent a care package with peanut butter and other healthy foods we couldn't find there. When we took possession of the package we noticed it had been rifled through and that a number of items were missing. We were both pissed and started to berate the postal employees. Us two hippies heaping upon them as much antiestablishment bullshit as we could come up with. When we left, I slammed the large glass door and it smashed into pieces. Oh shit. There was a big scene and the cops came and arrested me. They put me into the back of a jeep and we were driving off through some backstreets when the cops stopped to talk to some people they saw. We were just sitting there so I decided I would make a run for it; when I noticed they were deep into their conversation, I jumped out the back of the jeep and tried to make my getaway.

I was sprinting at top speed when I heard the *boom* of a gunshot ring out. I never froze so fast in my life. The head cop ran up to me and punched me in the face and I hit the ground. My advice to you if you are ever running from the cops and you hear a gunshot ring out is to stop running. You never know where that next gunshot may end up. They threw me in jail and the warden grilled me about how I had ended up the way I was. How I only owned one pair of jeans. How I had not cut my hair or beard for many years. He actually seemed perplexed about why and how I was living the way I was. As I sit here now and reminisce, I cannot even answer these questions myself. I had rebelled to such an extent against society that I had gone way overboard. We would not allow any mirrors in our home; maybe we were trying to prove that appearances were not important. This rebelliousness had really taken over and I am not sure from where it had come. The warden let me go the next day and told me to get myself together.

Ava and I were reunited and decided it was time to make our way down to Ecuador. We got onto the bus with all the possessions we owned, which fit into our backpacks. We were of the Jack Kerouac generation and lived day-to-day with no intention of garnering material possessions. We were "on the road" and trying to experience life to its fullest by seeing what we could learn and take away from our experiences.

We entered into Ecuador and the whole vibe of the people changed. It was very tranquilo and not as intense as Colombia. Being the simpleminded person that I was, I attributed this to the fact that the people there were not all jacked up on caffeine. We had read up about Ecuador and decided to make our way to a small town in the south of the country called Vilcabamba. Both Ava and I were interested in herbs and we had read about how the people there lived to be well over one hundred years old, so we wanted to see if we could discover some of the reasons for their longevity. We slowly made our way there with stops in the capital Quito, then Cuenca, then Loja, before reaching Vilcabamba.

We rented a house two hours by foot outside of town, way up in the valleys that surrounded Vilcabamba. We had no running water or electricity. There was no road. No cars. It was very remote, but it sat in a nice valley with pasture land all around it and some other small houses farther up the way.

We soon made friends with a man named Miguel Carpio who was 127 years old. Yes, that is correct. *National Geographic* eventually did a story on this place and a few books were also written about it. I remember one day in town when all the people over a hundred years old came in for a group portrait. It really was amazing. The town was on the eastern slope of the Andes and it felt like it was shielded. And the people all consumed food that was grown right there in that valley. Even the tobacco was grown there and they all rolled their own cigarettes. Nothing was produced from outside their area. It was a completely natural and healthy lifestyle and the people there only used herbal remedies and no medicines from outside of the region. The people of Vilcabamba drank lemon balm tea every day. Lemon balm is in the mint family and grows prolifically where there is water and spreads just like mint. There it was called lemoncilla, but it was the very same lemon balm. Needless to say, I always have a large patch of this in my yard and my family is always drinking it. And I give it away to friends so they can plant it. I also began to learn about herbs at this time through books like *A Modern Herbal* by Margaret Grieve from the early 1900s and *Back to Eden* by Jethro Kloss, and through the likes of Johnny Lovewisdom, who had settled in South America and made discoveries about the healing properties of papaya and raw foods when Western medicine couldn't treat his liver problems.

One day Ava and I noticed some San Pedro cacti growing on the hillside behind our house. This is a seven-sided cactus and is the one that contains mescaline. You have to carefully remove the waxy outer layer and spines and then make sure you do not cut into the white part that contains poisonous strychnine. It is only the thin green layer you want to ingest. I was of course known as The Doctor and I was studying herbs and plants and had probably prescribed one or two drugs in my time and always wanted to learn more about psychotropic substances. We knew the mescalito would induce vomiting as this was its way of cleansing the body. We slowly transcended into a very high and spiritual place. It was mellow but clearly psychedelic. Much different from the acid I had taken which always came on like a gangbuster and had a much less organic feel. As we sat outside our house on that hot sunny day getting higher and higher, who should show up but our landlord, who also happened to be a policeman. He was dressed in his green uniform and had decided to take a Sunday stroll up to the house to see how his tenants were doing. It didn't matter; we were in such a different place and not completely on the earth that we were able to just quietly sit and talk with him and let him know everything was okay. I am sure he felt it was unusual to have two hippie gringos renting this house so far up in the mountains, but maybe since he could not understand it he did not see any harm in it.

Many years later back in Washington, DC, I was working at the Warner Theatre and was backstage with the Jerry Garcia Band. They took The Doctor back to see Jerry and he was alone in a room with a small amp just noodling around on his electric guitar. Just the two of us hanging out. We were sitting there sniffing cocaine and rapping a little bit and it was a very cool vibe. Later, before the group went on stage, they gathered in a prayer circle and passed around a bottle of mescaline. I had been asked to be part of the circle and when the bottle was handed to me, I passed it on and did not partake. I have wondered what might have happened if I'd ended up tripping with Jerry and his Grateful Dead cohorts and if I would have been welcomed into their entourage and even worked for the band. Jah had a different destiny in store for me, and that would be the world of reggae and Jamaica and I am glad it turned out that way, as I am sure I would have burned out quickly in the world of the Dead.

Ava and I cut down a stalk of bananas from some land near us one time and hung it in our house. Late that night we heard some rocks landing on our roof. Then we heard people yelling from up above us. It was pitch-black in those mountains. Apparently we had inadvertently stolen the bananas, and the owners were furious. Plus, we were hippie foreigners and maybe we were not welcome. As terror rained down on our house that night, we were scared for our lives. We did not realize we had taken something from somebody. We had thought these were just plants that were growing naturally in the valley where we lived. I was screaming and saying I had a machete and I would fight to the death if need be. Believe me. That was a very long night and I learned an invaluable lesson that has stuck with me forever and that fits into the Rastafari lifestyle I eventually adopted: I will never take something that is not mine. I cannot steal. I cannot cheat. Those people were right to want to stone us for taking what was theirs. It still brings sorrow to me when I think of that night and how terrifying it was.

I am not sure if it was related to the stress of that night, but a week later both Ava and I came down with a severe case of hepatitis. We had been drinking the water from a stream in front of our house in which cows were defecating; this was the perfect scenario for contracting hepatitis. We should have been boiling the water but had neglected to do so and the result was yellow, jaundiced eyes and fingernails, urine the color of Coca-Cola, and total lethargy. We were very weak and needed to take care of ourselves so we went to the main hotel in town and were put up by an acquaintance named Raul Mendoza. We needed rest as we treated ourselves herbally, so we took a room there for over a month. We ate lots of papaya and drank lots of parsley tea. Parsley is a diuretic which makes you piss a lot, so I figured the more urine that went through and washed out the liver, the quicker we would get healed. We slowly began to eat, starting with potatoes and some other bland foods to get us back on track.

We were so naïve that when Raul had invited us to the hotel to recuperate, we did not realize we would be charged for our stay there. Raul ended up writing to my parents and demanding money for our stay, and there were even threats of him kidnapping us if we didn't pay—things had really gotten out of hand. My parents contacted the State Department and all these telexes alerted the US Embassy in Ecuador what was going on with us. I am not sure whatever happened with the outrageously high hotel bill, but it must have gotten paid somehow.

After we were well enough to hit the road, Ava and I packed up and headed north. We stopped in Quito, checked out the equator, where you can literally stand with a foot in each hemisphere, and we ended up staying at a yoga retreat just outside the city which was owned by an American who had at one time been Mr. Universe. The next day I visited the produce market with my long hair and beard and sandals and was given more fruits and vegetables than I could carry by the local women— they just kept coming up to me and piling them on. I had often used the phrase "Dios le paga" when people asked me to pay for what I was purchasing, as this literally meant that "God will pay." I guess that day it had finally borne fruit.

We wanted to get to know the Indian culture better and set out for Otavalo, which has a native population who are direct descendents of the Incas. There, we learned of three small villages nearby where the people were almost 100 percent Indios. We set out the next day for Ilumán. We asked some people if they knew of any houses for rent. They did not understand this concept at all but we were told that the Cordoba family had a vacant home. We met the family and told them we could pay them a fee for staying there. They showed us a small one-room mud house in the cornfield behind their primary home.

These people were pure Indian and some of the most beautiful humans I have ever met on the face of this Earth. They worshipped the sun and the rain and family and life. They were natural and lived from their land. Ava and I were still recovering from our hepatitis and needed to keep resting and taking things slow. The Cordoba family was incredibly welcoming to us and would include us at many of their dinners. We became friends with all of them. The women would carry large bundles of wood from up on the mountain to use for cooking. I remember one day going up there and offering to help carry down a bundle and completely collapsing under its weight. Everyone was laughing, including me, as I struggled to get back to my feet. I decided to leave the heavy lifting to the Indian women.

Life in Ilumán was an amazing experience. We saw how the Indians would weave their beautiful clothes and Tomás Cordoba showed me how to work the loom. Although he did not know what arithmetic was, the way he explained to me how he created his patterns into his weave was akin to a higher form of math. They grew vines of beans along rows of corn, and by eating corn and beans together they were consuming fifteen of the eighteen essential amino acids the body is looking for each day. They did not read this in a book; it just evolved over thousands of years and their bodies somehow let them know this is what they needed. As Ava and I were both vegetarians, we found this fascinating and we basked in the wonderment of their culture.

We learned some of the Incan native language Quechua. The Incas had a massive empire in South America in 1500 that reached all the way from Ecuador into Peru and Bolivia. Most people in Ilumán continued to speak Quechua and some did not even know Spanish. The Quechua language had no alphabet until 1975, though it is perhaps thousands of years old. When the conquistadores first came to South America, the Indians were astonished how when they dismounted their horses, one being turned into two. And likewise, the conquistadores were amazed at how advanced this culture was, with vast acres of agriculture and so much gold and beautiful art. The Europeans' lust for the gold and riches caused them to just take what they so desired and decimate an entire culture. And the Church with its missionaries played right along.

I remember one day the Cordobas returned from Otavalo on a Saturday, which was market day. The Catholic priests would always walk through the market with a collection plate and ask the people for money. The Cordobas asked me if I knew what "hell" was, and if such a place actually existed. They had been told by the priests that if they did not turn their lives over to Jesus and support the Church with monetary donations, they would end up in that horrible place. This made me so angry. Why did priests need to introduce this concept to these people who just wanted to live naturally? Who gave thanks for what they had and worshipped the sun and the rain and the simple things that made their lives work? I told them there was no such thing as hell and that the priest was a liar. Un mentiroso.

This incident later reminded me of the Bob Marley

song "Talkin' Blues," where he sings, *"And I feel like bombing a church / now that I know that the preacher is lying."* I hadn't previously understood the real meaning of these words, but now it made sense: how dare a religion lay such a heavy burden on these people. In every town we passed through, the church was always the most prominent building, right in the center of the village; the rebel in me was so disturbed that I realized I would never be able to reconcile the injustices perpetrated by the evil forces of Babylon and Rome and the Church. And now that the Church has been exposed for allowing the sodomizing of young boys by priests who have been denied the right to marry and enjoy a normal and healthy sex life, it makes me even angrier. And no, I do not believe Mary was a virgin. Anyone who has kids should know that.

After a month with the Cordobas, who ended up feeling like family due to their generosity and kindness, Ava and I decided to move on as our visa for Ecuador was going to expire and we needed to head back into Colombia. We left with great sadness in knowing our time there was over, but also with great joy for the experience we had been blessed with.

We had been told that when reentering Colombia it was very difficult to get a new three-month visa. We were also told that the border guards were open to bribes, so when one of them suggested he would give us a one-month visa, I asked him if it was possible to get a ninety-day visa if we paid an *impuesto* (tax). He looked at me and a small smile came across his face and he wrote down a number on the pad in front of him. I asked to borrow his pen and wrote another number that was much lower. I had become accustomed to bargaining in South America as a basic principal of transacting business. In the market you didn't pay the first price someone suggested. I have never gotten this bargaining aspect out of me and I can be a real pain in the ass when it comes to business negotiations. It's in my blood and I cannot deny it. We laughed and the guard accepted the impuesto I suggested and stamped us with ninety-day visas. Hola, Colombia. Adiós, Ecuador.

Ava and I wanted to go to San Agustín and eat the mushrooms and try to raise our consciousness. Some people may suggest this is just a fancy way of saying we wanted to get high, but in truth we were seeking spiritual enlightenment.

There were two ways to get to San Agustín. One was by taking a twelve-hour bus ride and the other was a hike through the jungle on a path that had been hand-cut by machete. There is a saying about choosing the path less traveled and I guess that is what Ava and I decided to do. There were road camps situated at either end of the path, as crews were working to eventually turn it into a road.

We set out to hitch a ride up to one of the road camps and were sitting by a high mountain pasture waiting for the next vehicle to pass. In many countries they do not really use bus stops. You just flag someone down and then figure out how much you will pay them to take you where you want to go. It's the same in rural Jamaica. Just flag them down and they will stop. We were sitting by that pasture smoking a joint when in front of us appeared an old man with sunken eyes on a white horse. He did not ride up to us, he just appeared. He started to warn us about the "masamores" and about "los nubes del norte" (the clouds from the north). He just kept shouting warnings to us and then called out, "Hasta luego!" and galloped off.

I turned to Ava and told her that we needed to heed his warnings. We didn't know what "masamores" were and we looked it up in our Spanish-English dictionary but could not find the word. His intense features, sunken eyes, white horse, and declaration that he would see us later had me convinced this was the angel of death. (He will see us all sooner or later, but this had me thinking about my mortality.) In truth, Ava and I were both un-settled by the occurrence as we waited for a vehicle to take us to the road camp so we could spend the night there and prepare for our hike the next day. Eventually, a truck carrying a bunch of workers stopped for us and carried us to the camp. We asked many people there about masamores, and were told it was a river we needed to cross on the path to San Agustín and that it was very dangerous and we would have to traverse it carefully.

The next morning we set out with a worker who showed us where the path started into the jungle. Ava and I were nervous but we knew it was our destiny to take this walk and we were not going to turn back. The jungle was thick and the path was narrow and muddy. About fifty yards in, we came to a fork. There was no in-dication of which way we should go. We walked a little ways in one direction and then decided it did not feel right so we turned around and took the other one. We walked and walked through the dense jungle. It started to rain, and the mud on the path got deeper. We made the mistake of smoking a joint and we became a little disoriented. There were more forks in the path, and the warnings from the angel of death still resonated in our brains. We saw large clawprints that resembled those of a fierce jungle animal. I took out my machete and kept on the lookout for anything wild. Soon we reached a raging river and slowly crossed it on a fallen tree, inching along on our butts. The rain came down heavier and the mud on the path kept getting deeper. After many hours of walking, we were both scared that we were lost.

Our fear gave way to comfort after a while when we heard the sound of equipment from afar. It was the sound of civilization. Of bulldozers working to clear the land and build the road that would connect the two sides of the path. Somewhere in the distance we knew we would find the next road camp and complete our journey. We picked up our pace as we were desperate to get out of that jungle. Nearing the spot where the bulldozers were working, we sank to our knees in a large pool of mud. As I reached the bank on the other side, I turned around and saw that Ava was stuck. She could not move. I managed to slowly pull her to safety and it was at this point that we realized we had just crawled through a pool of quicksand.

We sat on the bank trembling and shouting for help—"Ayúdame! Ayúdame!" The bulldozers were pushing the mud down the hillside into the pool below. Finally, one of the drivers heard us and came down and helped carry us up the hill. We were taken over to the road camp and given some dry clothes and hot coffee and we huddled together and talked about how we had escaped from the angel of death and that it was not the masamores we had needed to fear but instead the quick-sand. We were so glad to be alive and back with people and out of that jungle. The people at the road camp told us of another couple who had left from their side and had come back out three days later after getting lost and were totally out of their minds and had to be hospital-ized. The jungle is not for the faint of heart.

Ava and I thanked our lucky stars and left the next morning for San Agustín. We were in guerilla territory here, as they were known to frequent these mountains and seek help from the farmers. There had been an on-going struggle within Colombia for over one hundred years—this is part of what inspired Gabriel García Márquez to write his famous book *One Hundred Years of Solitude*. The rebels were known as the Fuerzas Armadas Revolucionarias de Colombia (FARC) and were fighting to liberate the people. Kidnapping, cocaine trafficking, and various acts of espionage were their forte. All to raise money to support the revolution. In any event, we settled into our house and got to know our neighbors.

We traveled by bus out to a large cow pasture near kilometer nine on the road outside of San Agustín. This field was well known as a place you could find plenty psilocybin mushrooms growing from the cow turds. We carried our basket with a cloth laid inside and began carefully picking mushrooms. We were both adept at picking the right ones: bright orange tops with a purple ring around the stem where the spores had fallen.

As we took our time and walked through the cow fields gathering mushrooms, we ate a few to help get in touch with our surroundings. I remember looking across the valley and seeing these bright green moun-

tains as they would change hues and feeling so peaceful
and so connected and disconnected to the Earth all at
the same time. Maybe that is why they call it a trip. On
the bus back from this field we were stopped by gueril-
las and searched, and some people were asked to get
off for questioning and some items were taken from the
luggage racks above the seats. It was all very strange but
the bus ended up moving on.

That night Ava and I decided to make cream of mushroom soup. We cooked in clay pots on a wood fire and
ate from gourds. We were trying to be as natural as possible. We got some milk from a farmer nearby and some
green beans to put in as well. We added around fifty
mushrooms that night and it was way, way too much. I
thought I was going to die. I cried out for my mother. I
cried out for God. Ava and I kept each other from sleeping. There were some New Zealanders who had stayed
with us and they had a little monkey and it ate a mushroom, got all excited, then went to sleep and never woke
up. We knew we had to stay awake if we were going to
make it through the night. Somehow we did. Another
long, eventful night way up in the mountains of South
America.

Ultimately, during our back-and-forth adventures between Colombia and Ecuador, we spent thirteen straight
months there. We had been disenchanted with America,
with the Vietnam War, and with tricky Dick Nixon. I
remember one day in Vilcabamba, Ecuador, being told
that my president had resigned. Yes, Nixon had finally
stepped down.

We returned to the States with a severe case of culture shock. Seeing all these suburban kids lined up at bus stops when in my mind I was remembering the days on the river eating mangoes and swimming. Ava and I ended up renting a basement apartment by Dupont Circle in downtown DC. I got a job working at a bookstore and read as much as I could and tried to increase my knowledge.

One evening during my dinner break I was in a park near work and I met a couple from Colombia. Eventually our discussion came around to marijuana and I suggested we walk up to my apartment so I could give them some. When we arrived, Ava was in bed with another guy. Everyone was shocked. I could not handle it mentally and things took a really bad turn the next week when I came down with the clap. Gonorrhea. I can tell you that if you have never had it, it is not fun. Not fun at all and quite painful. I will spare you the details but I would not wish it on my worst enemy. This was the beginning of the end for Ava and me, and when I told you earlier that there were good things about being with a nymphomaniac and some not-so-good things, this is what I was talking about.

South America will always hold a special place in my heart. Many years after I started RAS Records, I had Freddie McGregor sing a reggae version of "Guantanamera," which was released on the Phillips label in Colombia and became a hit, and we did some touring there to support the single. And I also spent much time in Chile later, producing Gondwana and helping to start a local reggae and Rasta movement. My ability to speak Spanish has served me well as I continue to enjoy conversing with the many Latinos I encounter on a daily basis here in the US.

When I tell people I went to Colombia after high school, they assume I mean Columbia University in New York, and I never bother to correct them. I certainly got an education there and somehow graduated with flying colors. The impact this had on my life is monumental and has taught me how to take care of myself in even the most difficult of situations. Just think if I had just gone off to college instead.

RAS RECORDS

The race is not for the swift but for those who can endureth.
—RAS Records motto

Real Authentic Sound

I had been doing my Doctor Dread show *Night of the Living Dread* on WHFS radio for almost a year, and although I was feeling really good about spreading the reggae vibe to the greater Washington, DC area, I was starting to think about ways that I could be even more instrumental in expanding the reach of this music I loved so dearly. It seemed to me there was a lack of distribution of these great records I would bring up from Jamaica and that Americans did not have access to. I had been working with my oldest brother Steve in the seafood business as my deejay gig did not really pay the bills.

Steve had started a seafood company in upstate New York and I had begun selling fish in the DC area. He would send down a truckful of fish once a week, and as the business grew, he decided to close up shop in the

Catskills and take the business full-time here in Washington. We were supposedly partners but we had some fundamental differences in how we felt the business should be run. This frustration caused me to quit and he told me that a boss could not quit his own company. Well, I had other fish to fry and decided I was going to do what I loved—not what other people thought I should do with my life.

I was hosting my reggae show on Sunday nights and was getting more involved in Jamaica, Rastafari, and the DC Jamaican community. I went for it full tilt: it was reggae or bust. And although many family members tried to convince me to go back into business with my brother, I stood firm. In fact, this is when I consider that I became a man. I would make my own decisions and live with the consequences. Do with my life what my heart told me to do. I was twenty-seven years young.

Many of the large record labels were three-letter acronyms: CBS, WEA, EMI, BMG. I settled on the name RAS (Real Authentic Sound). And, come to think of it, there is the Power of the Trinity at work again! And although I did not know much about music publishing, I somehow knew it was important, so I started Tafari Music as the companion publishing entity to RAS. RasTafari. I liked it. I later learned that *Tafari* is the Amharic word for *Creator*, which is a relevant name since the songwriter creates music. And the word *Ras* means *Head*, which signifies that RAS Records would become the top reggae label, while having the double meaning of the name that Haile Selassie I was given when he was crowned emperor of Ethiopia. I knew very little about this business, but I was determined to spread the music and culture of reggae far and wide. Right across the whole planet.

I figured the first thing I needed to do was connect with an audience, so I set up a distribution company in the basement of my home in Chevy Chase, Maryland. Knowing that I could not do this alone, I partnered up with David Pansegrouw, a Vermonter who shared my love of reggae. He came down to DC and we worked day and night packing up vinyl and sending it out to record stores across America. I had the sister of my girlfriend make up a catalog based on the records in my personal collection and she also drew for me the now famous RAS lion that became the company's logo. I started to make contact with the labels on all the records in my collection and told them of my plans to begin distributing reggae in America. Labels like Trojan, Greensleeves, VP, Top Ranking, Tuff Gong, Dynamic, and Sonic Sounds. Even the big ones like Island and CBS. I resolved to have the most complete catalog of reggae available to anyone in America (or worldwide) who wanted it. I planned to travel to Jamaica and start making deals with manufacturers and small independent record labels.

Soon, RAS was gaining a reputation as the go-to company to find reggae. Even Bunny Wailer began selling me his vinyl pressings direct and I was able to get these to accounts who had no other way of obtaining them. I would load up with LPs every time I returned from Jamaica. It was backbreaking work but I persisted, and there was never a question that it would get done.

Sadly, the biggest break young RAS Records got was the passing of Bob Marley on May 11, 1981. Island Records owned the Marley catalog in America, but when

Bob passed they were in the process of switching distribution from WEA to PolyGram. So for a period there were no Bob Marley records available in America (it was all vinyl in those days; the CD had not yet been invented). Except that RAS had a whole wall of shelves filled with Bob Marley albums that had been pressed by the Tuff Gong label in Jamaica.

In other words, at that point in time, the only place in the whole of America you could buy Bob Marley from was RAS. The orders started to pour in. Records chains from the Midwest. California. New York. All over. We could barely keep these in stock, but because we had built up a good relationship with Tuff Gong in Jamaica, they kept shipping us loads of music. I would drive out to the airport and clear these myself through customs, and David and I would then unpack them, put the records on the shelves, and repack them to go out to our customers.

And while they were buying all these Bob Marley records, we took the opportunity to turn them on to other great reggae we were distributing. I felt most of the record stores knew very little about the genre and would fill their reggae bins with whatever they had received from the distributors; it was like they were just pushing product. When someone discovered Bob Marley and got turned on to reggae, they would go to stores and usually only find this watered-down crap catered to the American market. I was out to change this. I would fill the reggae bins with the Real Authentic Sound of Jamaica so that when the customer took a chance and bought a reggae record, they would love it and become a reggae fan. Not just a Bob Marley fan. We knew good reggae and we had a plan to help this music break in America.

We quickly outgrew the confines of my basement and rented a small warehouse in Kensington, Maryland. David and I parted ways early on, as maybe I was too ambitious and was pushing too hard. While David always took a methodical approach, I was impulsive and relied on faith, and my gut reactions and vibes formed the basis of my decisions moving forward.

Peter Broggs

One day I was outside of Gregory Isaacs's African Museum record shop on Chancery Lane in downtown Kingston. Not many white guys hung around these places, but by this time I was comfortable in any part of Kingston, and in Jamaica in general. Singer Peter Broggs was hanging out there and I told him I loved to play his music on my radio show back in the States. He did not believe me. He said no one knew him outside of Jamaica. I sang a few of his songs and he got a real big smile on his face and soon we were laughing together. I told him I had written some songs that I would like him to record. He took me around the corner to a private place and asked me to sing them to him. He said he loved them and suggested we do a whole album together.

As it turned out, Peter was close with a good friend of mine, Bongo from Negril. Broggs was born over by Lucea and knew Bongo from when they were youths. Westmoreland Parish was now known for producing the best sinse in all of Jamaica, and Bongo had the best of the best. A very dark-skinned dread with massive locks, Bongo had a good heart and was cool in how he dealt with people. In my early days of going to Jamaica, I would always chill in Negril and hang with Bongo and we became close friends and remain so to this day.

The first time I took my brother Steve, his wife Judy, and their two kids to Jamaica, we stayed in one of these all-inclusive fancy hotels on the beach in Negril. I had gone to visit Bongo and when I was leaving his yard on the beach, the police stopped me and saw I had some weed. When they realized it was from Bongo they just looked at him and said, "Oh. A you, Bongo, sorry for the disturbance," and let me drive on. They probably showed up later to get their little food money from Bongo, as in Jamaica this is how things sometimes work. One hand washes the other.

When I got back to the hotel, Peter Broggs had come to visit. Now, as I mentioned earlier, in Jamaica they do not like when the natives visit with the tourists at their hotels. Especially at the all-inclusives. And seeing a dread like Broggs hanging out with us on the beach and around the pool probably had their panties in a snit. But Broggs was my friend and why should a dread or anyone else be treated in an inferior manner to the next person? We went back to my room and burned a little spliff and the next thing we know the hotel manager (some white ex-Nazi or something from Germany, no lie) and his goons were pounding on the door. I hid the weed and opened the door and they could smell what had been going on. By this time my brother and his wife and kids had come back to the room. Turning to his help, the manager commanded, "You have my permission, search the room!" Well, they spent about an hour tearing that room apart but I had gotten very good at stashing my stash so they never found it and became extremely frustrated. They made Broggs leave the premises and told me to watch myself. Fuck them.

Bongo agreed to put up 50 percent of the money to record the album with Broggs. I hired the Roots Radics band at the recommendation of Broggs and rented out time at Channel One studios on Maxfield Avenue in Kingston. Channel One had become home to Sly & Robbie, and at the time was turning out the toughest rockers inna yard. Sound is an interesting thing. When you find a room with the right vibes and warmth it can add substantially to the overall sound of a record. Just like Studio One, there was a sound to the music recorded there that in some intangible way added to its feel. I am sure it was the same at Sun, Motown, and Chess studios in America.

Bongo was there and Broggs ended up recording the two songs I had written, as well as a number of his own to finish out the LP. I remember having Scientist mix the record over at Tuff Gong. All within a one-week time period in Jamaica. Scientist also did a wicked dub mix of "International Farmer," which became an international anthem for Broggs, and we put both the vocal and dub mix together on the album. RAS was now officially a record label. This hard-core first LP on RAS was titled *Rastafari Liveth!*, and we had the lyrics translated into three languages—French, Spanish, and German—which I printed on the inner sleeve of the album along with the English.

For me it was all about spreading the message of Rastafari to the world. I did not really have the money to manufacture this first LP. Color separations, printing jackets, making metal stampers to press the LPs, and then actually pressing them cost thousands of dollars. I knew next to nothing about running a record label, but I had recorded an album and I liked it and wanted to get it released. I had taken the cover photo of Broggs over at King Tubby's studio and helped design the cover. I had done just about everything myself and was ready to sell my Volvo to raise the funds to press the LP. My color separator talked me out of this and told me to "never sell your car to pay for a record." I listened to him and eventually found a way to come up with the money to have my first record pressed and delivered in 1982. RAS 3001.

The problem was that when I went to sell it, all the stores told me they had never heard of Peter Broggs and did not believe any of their customers would buy the record. Never one to take no for an answer, I told them that no one had heard of Bob Marley when he released his first record and that they needed to give Broggs a chance. I did not give up. I saw that to press an album cost around one dollar, and you could sell it for eight. I had also gotten a taste of what it was to be a producer and witness the magic that was created in a recording studio. For me there was no turning back. Forward ever. Backward never.

Freddie McGregor

I next signed Freddie McGregor to a three-record deal. I was beginning to learn more about the business and would attend music conventions and read *Billboard* and other music publications cover to cover. My whole life was now RAS Records. Day and night. Every waking moment. I advanced Freddie $10,000 for that first LP. In my neophyte mentality I believed that Freddie could be the next Bob Marley. Little did I know that there could never be another Bob Marley . . .

In any event, Freddie delivered the album *Come On Over*, and that was RAS 3002, released in 1983. Jet Star, the main distributor for reggae in England and Europe, ordered one thousand copies alone. Evidently Freddie was very popular in the UK, and this LP was considered to be a top-quality production. The next week they called me and reordered a thousand more!

But about six months later I got a call from a Jamaican named Linval Thompson. He explained that he had paid for and produced this album for Freddie, and that Freddie had taken a cassette and copied it to a two-track tape and sent it to me, and that Linval was the owner of this master. He told me he was going to sue little RAS Records and take over the company for himself. I can't say I blame him for feeling this way. But I knew I had to stick up for myself. I explained that I had a signed contract with Freddie and had advanced him good money for the LP, and that I had no intention of stepping down. I had to defend myself. And although it introduced an element of being wary about dealing with artists (thanks, Freddie), I knew there was much more in store for RAS Records and I would not let this deter me from my mission of spreading reggae and Rastafari as far and wide as possible. I guess I figured Freddie and Linval would work this out, and that if Linval wanted to release this LP too, I could not stop him.

Melodians

My next project was a recording I did with the Melodians at Lion and Fox Studios in Washington, DC. This was the first harmony trio I worked with and the group was well-known internationally for their classic "Rivers of Babylon" from the sound track to *The Harder They Come*. I also loved some of their early rootsy classics and was excited to work with them, as I found each of them to be very nice and cool to deal with. They explained to me that not all the music I produced had to be serious and about Rastafari and the message I was hoping to get out. That people want to relax. To enjoy life. That music could be about love and emotions and the happy side of life. That people want to have a good time. Go out dancing. Drink a little. You know, *"Do a little dance, make a little love, get down tonight."*

They were right. I was probably taking myself too seriously and I needed to lighten up. I will always be grateful to them for letting me know that life is one big road with lots of signs.

Around the same time, I first met these two teenagers—Johnny Temple and Bobby Sullivan from the punk group Soulside—outside a Toots & the Maytals show in DC. Johnny is now the publisher of Akashic Books, the company that released the book you are holding in your hands. This is further proof that you should always treat all people well and with dignity and respect, as the circle of life will often bring you back into contact with those who you have met in the past.

Don Carlos and Michigan & Smiley
I next traveled to Jamaica to record two albums. The RAS label was gaining recognition, and I was beginning to set up licensing deals in England, Europe, Japan, and even Africa. My vision was starting to unfold before my

very eyes and I knew that Jah was playing an important role in the fulfillment of prophecy. Jah guide every time.

I loved the singer Don Carlos and also wanted to do an album with Michigan & Smiley. I had played lots of Don Carlos on my old radio show and was excited to have the opportunity to work with him in the studio. I booked out Tuff Gong on Hope Road and again called on the Roots Radics to lay down the rhythm tracks. The Radics were becoming my go-to band and were instrumental in getting me the hard-core reggae sound I was looking for.

We laid down the tracks for the LP *Just a Passing Glance* and I was blown away. Don had such a pure voice and his whole being was engulfed in Rastafari. Always humble and giving praises to Jah. Carlton Barrett (from the Wailers) played drums on some of these tracks and it added another strong one-drop element to the music. And recording in the home of Bob Marley was a vibe all unto itself. Errol Brown, who continues to work as the sound engineer for Ziggy Marley when he tours, as well as Rebelution, and who recorded and mixed most of Bob's albums, was the recording engineer for both the Don Carlos and Michigan & Smiley LPs. Errol and I remain close to this day and I always cook him up some fish to eat when he passes through DC on tour.

On the international front, Don Carlos was huge in South Africa. Reggae resonated deeply in the country, since Jamaican artists were among the first musicians to sing out against apartheid. I was offered big money to license Don Carlos for release in South Africa (and RAS was the first label to be offered the singer Lucky Dube), but I had to refuse this and other deals since I had made the conscious decision to boycott all business in the country till apartheid was abolished—I couldn't live with even a dollar of tax money from record sales supporting the government.

To the best of my knowledge, Michigan & Smiley were the original deejay duo to emerge on the scene. Before Run-DMC and all the other rap duos out there. They did a wicked LP for Coxsone Dodd on the Studio One label, and their vocal interplay and lyrical exchanges created a unique vibe. They had come to my hotel room in Jamaica one evening with a yellow legal pad with some lyrics written out. Songs like "Blackness Awareness," with the lyrics, *"You try to take my history and destroy my soul."* Some pretty heavy shit. I loved it. This was real talent and not just some gimmick a deejay had come up with. We recorded the *Sugar Daddy* LP in one week, and Errol Brown mixed it. No slacking. RAS 3004, released in 1983. The title track, "Sugar Daddy," went on to become a number-one hit song in Jamaica on the RAS label. A 7" single selling well over twenty thousand copies. How cool is that?

Michigan & Smiley were to appear at the big Reggae Sunsplash festival that year in Montego Bay. It was my plan to bring down cases of the Sugar Daddy candies to throw out to the crowd from the stage when they performed that song. I had learned from a good friend the art of becoming invisible, and would often resort to this tactic when passing through customs and at other times when it was necessary. I will not explain in detail what this means, but I am sure those of you who are also versed in this art will fully overstand.

I had given Brent Dowe from the Melodians the

money to press the single there in Jamaica. One day he called me up and said, "Guess what, Doc? I've opened up a record store on Slipe Road where the old Tony Robinson store used to be. And I've decided to call it RAS Records." All I could do was laugh; he never paid me a cent for those singles or any of the subsequent business we did together, but I didn't get bent out of shape over it since I knew that at least I was able to help Brent put a little food on his table. And I certainly had no intention of suing him like so many other record labels would have done. It was just live and let live. Seen?

RAS made its first video for the song "Sugar Daddy," and we did it with a company that wanted to get into the music video business so they didn't charge us anything. All we had to do was to get Michigan & Smiley to the US and they would do the rest. The video became a big hit as well, and RAS was making some new waves around the world. It was at this time that I also began working with the photographer Tommy Noonan. He took the cover photo for *Sugar Daddy* and he and I also went into the Waterhouse ghetto of Kingston with some high-powered strobe lights to shoot the cover for the Don Carlos collection *Raving Tonight*. I licensed the songs from the Palmer brothers in England, who had produced these tracks for their Negus Roots label.

That night in Waterhouse was wild, as we had crowds of people who all came out to be with Don Carlos and his close brethren and backup singer Gold. The energy was fierce, and although Waterhouse is considered one of the rougher areas of Kingston, we felt completely safe as Don and Gold ran things and vouched for

Tommy and me. It hit me that the same tunes of Don that I had loved to play on the radio were now coming out on the RAS label, and again I felt that somehow a prophecy was being fulfilled. I could not explain how these things ended up happening but I had the feeling that Jah had something to do with it.

During this time I was also working closely with album designer and artist Dick Bangham. Dick was well known in music circles in DC and designed lots of covers for local artists. He was adept with an airbrush and could create all kinds of different images on an album cover. This was before we had personal computers and most album covers were done with real art created by real artists. Tommy had taken a photo of Don Carlos walking past a redbrick wall in the Georgetown neighborhood in Washington, DC. There were some white flower petals from a dogwood tree on the ground that day and Tommy just caught a vibe as Don walked along. This would become the cover photo for the album *Just a Passing Glance*. Dick had airbrushed an image of Selassie I onto a piece of clear plastic and superimposed it on the wall next to Don. It was not feeling quite right to me and I suggested Dick move the image of Selassie up so that half of His head was above the wall and half on the wall. More like a spirit than a painting on a wall. When Dick showed me what he had done, my body filled with chills. It was the perfect fit for a song that described how Don had a "passing glance" of Rastafari. The artwork conveyed it perfectly, and to this day it is my favorite RAS album cover.

And maybe it was that song that somehow caused me to sight up His Imperial Majesty Emperor Haile Selassie I the First. King of Kings. Lord of Lords. Conquering Lion from the Tribe of Judah. I can never forget that day. I was walking along Trafalgar Road in Kingston. It was a bright, sunny day. All of a sudden my whole body was filled with Haile Selassie I. It just filled me up like a light taking over my body and spirit. I can't explain it, but I remember it like it happened this morning and I still get goose bumps when I think about it. And no one can tell I and I that even though I am a white man and do not have dreads that I cannot give praises to His Majesty. NOBODY. And I and I do give praises every day. And I will let you in on something: *I and I* is an important part of the Rastafari belief. It means that I-self has a one-on-one relationship with His Majesty and with God. A personal connection. This is why Rastafari is so individualized. I am sure many religions may have the same precept in their doctrines, but for I and I this is I truth. Seen?

So not only was RAS putting out some kick-ass reggae, we were also doing some high-quality packaging. I knew I had to compete with all the major labels and that as an independent I was more agile and could move in ways the giants could not. Many people believe the music industry is a sleazy and dirty business, but I can assure you that many independent labels were borne out of one person's passion to produce and expose a specific kind of music dear to his or her heart. Ahmet Ertegun of Atlantic. Bruce Iglauer of Alligator. Moe Asch of Folkways. Ian MacKaye and Jeff Nelson of Dischord. Ken, Marianne, and Bill of Rounder Records. The list is endless. All of these people were just into the music, and being profitable was a necessity for keeping a business alive so they could make records they loved and that hopefully the public would love as well. It was the same for RAS. We never had any money in the bank; all our funds were used to produce the next album. Or make a video. Or do some promotion to help sales.

Now that RAS had established itself as a major reggae force and had developed a reputation for treating the artists with respect and not ripping them off, many musicians and producers began to approach us. Our distribution division had also grown significantly as a young guy I hired named Steve Cornwell built our relationships with other labels to help distribute their music as well. I have always believed that competition is healthy and it forces you to be a better company. And instead of focusing on what other labels were doing, I always tried to just forge my own path through the jungle. To be a trendsetter. A trailblazer. To come up with new ideas for producing, promoting, and distributing. To leave no stone unturned. In Jamaica they say that "one-one coco fill a basket." This means that if you pick one coconut at a time, eventually you will fill up your basket. I took that same approach. One coconut at a time.

Eek-A-Mouse

Tony Welch and George Michalow at the Fast Lane booking agency each had some Eek-A-Mouse tracks, so we put them together and released *Assassinator* (RAS 3006). I always looked for unique qualities in an artist, and at 6'6" above sea level, Eek-A-Mouse claimed to be the tallest entertainer in the world. He had a "singjay" style that was his and his alone (although he did spawn some copycats along the way). He had scored a cross-over pop hit in England with the song "Wa-Do-Dem" and had begun to build a large fanbase on both sides of the pond. (England was a significant reggae market, as many Jamaican immigrants had settled there after World War II and Jamaica remained a British colony until its independence in 1962; there was even a time when Jamaicans could travel to England without a visa, though those days are now long gone.) I ended up producing a few Eek-A-Mouse releases myself, and on his last CD for RAS I wrote many of the lyrics while my friend Ayoola from Nigeria created all the rhythms on his computer.

But the Mouse lost control at some point, and his behavior grew increasingly erratic. Mouse was in and out of jail, often calling me for bail, and was working out fiercely at the gym and nicknamed himself "Schwartza-nigger." He ended up stranded in Brazil for over a year at some point and ran up an astronomical hotel bill. The next thing I heard was that he was in some town in Paraguay, just across the border from Brazil. I read in a Jamaican newspaper that Eek had been extradited to the US to face rape charges for an incident that happened after a show he performed in North Carolina. If someone is going to track you down to a small, dusty, rundown border town in Paraguay and get you extradited to the States, it must be some pretty serious shit.

In 1988 I decided to put together an album of Christmas songs featuring the RAS family of artists. The vibes between myself and the musicians were like family, and having a reggae Christmas album would add a new twist for the holiday season. Freddie McGregor helped me produce and put the album together, which featured Don Carlos, Freddie, Michigan & Smiley, J.C. Lodge, and Eek-A-Mouse (*"On the night before Christmas all through the house, not a creature was stirring, only I, Eek-A-Mouse"*), among others. This album became enormously successful worldwide, including licensing deals in New Zealand, Africa, Canada, England, Europe, Japan, and South America. Even Tuff Gong in Jamaica. What a blessing, especially to know it had been made through the support and love the artists had for a young RAS Records.

Many producers also approached RAS about releasing their CDs. Gussie Clarke came to us with the Gregory Isaacs LP *Private Beach Party* (RAS 3007). Gussie had opened a studio on Slipe Road and was becoming the hottest producer in Jamaica. He was a businessman to the core, and it was always a pleasure to deal with someone who was straight and understood the runnings of the music industry. He later licensed RAS the *Red Rose* album from Gregory with the massive hit "Rumors," and both of these releases turned out to be huge for us. RAS was now a household name within the Jamaican and mainstream reggae communities.

When Gussie built his new Anchor Works studio on Windsor Road, I advanced him $5,000 to help with his costs. He never forgot that and always treated me well. Anchor became the studio where I did 90 percent of my recording in Jamaica since Tuff Gong had closed down their studio and turned the property into the Bob Marley Museum. And Gussie's studio soon became the most renowned place for recording and mixing in Jamaica. I also got him a deal with the Ampex tape company, where he became the exclusive distributor of recording tape for

Ampex for the whole of the Caribbean. I know Gussie made lots of money from this, though I never asked to be cut into the deal. In fact, when I do something for someone, or lend a helping hand, all I really would like in return is respect. But if you disrespect me, that is another story.

Brigadier Jerry
RAS also had the honor of releasing the first Brigadier Jerry LP, *Jamaica Jamaica*, in 1985. Briggy was my all-time favorite deejay. He would often sing at Jah Love dances and his live cassette tapes were coveted by hard-core fans all over the island. But he would not record in the studio; it was like a sacred act that you could only catch Briggy live, which was perhaps part of the mystique and allure that kept fans coming out. The Jah Love dances were a big support mechanism for the Twelve Tribes organization, of which Briggy was a member. Belcher owned Jah Love Sound and Ilawi was the selector, and together they produced the first Briggy LP. I believe Neville Lee from Sonic Sounds recommended RAS as the label to release the album; what an honor—people knew there must be something special about us if we had been selected to release this album by Briggy. Later Damian Marley used the refrain from "Jamaica Jamaica" in his monster hit "Welcome to Jamrock," and acknowledged that it was from Briggy that he got some of the lyrics and melody.

RAS became a flurry of activity. We moved to a larger warehouse, hired more employees. We were firing on all cylinders. Our distribution side put out these amazing catalogs and people all over the world would order their reggae from us. I began to tour RAS artists in America as the RAS Posse, with a mix of artists all backed by Freddie's Studio One Band. Freddie McGregor with Peter Broggs, Michigan & Smiley, and J.C. Lodge. It was all about the vibes and spreading the gospel of reggae across this great nation of ours.

We were the first Jamaican artists to ever go into Hopiland and spend time with the Hopis. That began a long personal relationship with me and the Hopis that opened up the way for many reggae artists to play music there. The Hopis are a special people and their reservation is sacred. No photos or alcohol are allowed. They have inhabited the same mesas for over nine hundred years; they were a peaceful tribe and did not go to war with the other Native American tribes. They could relate to how Jamaicans had been taken by force from Africa to live in a slave colony the same way that many Native Americans had been forced off their land to live on reservations. We established a cultural connection: Hopis and Jamaicans, brought together through reggae music.

Black Uhuru

Another monumental event that happened during the first years of RAS was the signing of Black Uhuru. They had just won the first reggae Grammy for their album *Anthem*, but lead singer Michael Rose had left the group. It made me wonder if winning a Grammy was a blessing or a curse. I knew Uhuru well and bandleader Duckie Simpson called me and told me about the situation; he said that Junior Reid had now taken over as lead singer, and that the group wanted to sign with RAS Records. I was on a plane to Jamaica within two days of that phone call. I have always said that when opportunity knocks at your door, you have to at least open it and see what it is all about—and we agreed on a two-record deal.

Island Records had spent quite a bit of money promoting Black Uhuru to a mainstream rock audience, including some touring with the Police and Rolling Stones. Sly & Robbie were an integral part of the Black Uhuru sound and they had made a commitment to stay on with the group with Junior Reid as lead singer. Vocalist Puma Jones was still part of the group too, and the first recordings I heard with this new lineup all sounded really good. This was a major signing for RAS and we were now the largest reggae label in the world. Do you hear me? In the whole fucking world! All my distributors who had been taking their sweet-ass time to pay me all of sudden paid up everything as I solicited them for copies of our new Black Uhuru album, *Brutal*.

Arthur Baker was the hottest producer/engineer/mixer in the entire music business in those days, and we approached him about remixing and adding some production touches to the "Great Train Robbery" song from the *Brutal* album. Cindy Abrams, a young woman who worked at RAS in those days, helped make the connection with Arthur, who had never worked with a reggae act—though he had recently completed projects with the Rolling Stones, Madonna, and Cyndi Lauper. I figured he would think this was a cool foray out of his normal comfort zone. It worked. He agreed to do the project for a minimal fee as he was very interested in checking out the reggae vibes and the music. So Uhuru and I all headed up to New York and began work at his studio. We voiced and mixed the track there and did a number of overdubs, especially keyboards and percussion. Arthur was extremely talented and I learned a great deal about studio technique from watching him work.

This was new territory for me, and I've got to admit it sounded wicked. The song went on to hit the British pop charts (a first for RAS) and was released as a single internationally. It was at this time that I got a call from Virgin Records in England. They told me they thought the pairing of Black Uhuru with Arthur Baker was "brilliant," and they would love to get some of their artists connected with him as well. They also told me how much they loved the RAS Christmas LP and they wanted to distribute it in England. I explained that I had an excellent relationship with Greensleeves and they were doing a great job on "Great Train Robbery" and that I had already licensed them the RAS Christmas LP. When Virgin realized they could not get what they wanted from RAS, they suddenly changed their tune from being warm and friendly to threatening. They twisted things around in an attempt to put me on the defensive. I had gotten my first taste of how the big record companies like to bully us small independents.

We had done a deal with Nippon Crown in Japan for the release of *Brutal*. They had agreed to ship us spools of five hundred CDs so we could assemble them in our warehouse in the US. This was the first reggae compact disc to ever hit the market—though it was released as a blister pack, the most un-eco-friendly and unnecessary piece of plastic ever made. The album went on to earn a Grammy nomination in 1987 and Black Uhuru and I all traveled out to Los Angeles to take part in the ceremonies, which was another first for myself and RAS Records. Sitting in the crowd that night with the curtains drawn on the stage, we began to hear music; when the curtains flew up, Ladysmith Black Mambazo were lifting up their feet as Paul Simon launched into his hit "Diamonds on the Soles of Her Shoes." What a kick-ass way to start off the Grammys. *Graceland* won Album of the Year, and although Black Uhuru did not take home the Grammy for *Brutal*, it was still a great trip I will always cherish. We also released an instrumental *Brutal Dub* album that was nominated the next year for a Grammy.

I had some black-and-white album jackets printed for *Positive Dub* (the dub version of our next full-length Black Uhuru release, *Positive*), and we laid them down in the parking lot outside RAS and spray-painted them red, yellow, and green, then let them dry in the sun. Each cover was a unique, one-of-a-kind painting, and it was also a way for me to give some of my staff a break from the mundane work of packing up boxes.

Puma was a perfectionist in the studio, which is something I've always found bothersome. Many artists can be perfectionists, but as a producer, I was always out to capture the magic of the moment. Besides, only Jah is perfect, so why seek what we cannot achieve? Tragically, Puma passed away from cancer in 1990 shortly after the Grammy trip. RAS did one more album with Black Uhuru with a new female harmony singer Duckie brought into the group, but it turned out to be a short run.

Coxsone Dodd
Around this same time I negotiated with Coxsone Dodd at Studio One to start a joint label. I came up with the

name RASSO (Real Authentic Sound of Studio One); RAS was the largest distributor of Studio One records and Mr. Dodd and I had built up a solid relationship. I still believe Studio One released the best music to ever come out of Jamaica and I tried to emulate Dodd by producing songs that would survive the test of time. Music that would endure forever and sound just as good twenty years down the road. Our motto had become, "The race is not for the swift but for those who can endureth." RAS was in it for the long run. It was not a get-rich-quick scheme. Not a hustle like so many I had seen enter the business before then quickly backing out.

The first release on the RASSO label was called *All on the Same Rhythm*, which had ten tracks on the "Pass the Kutchie" rhythm. I had always loved the Freddie McGregor song "Bobby Bobylon," and this led to the idea of putting out all these different Studio One selections Coxsone had in his vaults that had been recorded on the same rhythm. Fifteen years later this concept would become all the rage as producers began loading up all the latest rhythms with a myriad of artists to see if anything would stick to the wall.

Rounder Records, which had an affiliated reggae label called Heartbeat, was amazed I had gotten Dodd to agree to a joint venture. And even though Heartbeat and RAS were technically competitors, we both distributed each other's records and had a solid relationship. I always loved Duncan Browne who ran the whole Rounder group and owned 25 percent of Heartbeat. Duncan and I were talking on the phone about the Coxsone deal one day and I joked, "If you think the deal is so great, why don't you just buy RAS Records and then you could have the deal for yourself?" Duncan called me back the very next day and asked me, "How much?"

Well, truth be told, I was only paying myself $35,000 a year as I did not want to bleed the company to death, and we never had any money in the bank since we were always reinvesting in signing new artists and producing new records. I was also over thirty years old, had met a girl I was crazy in love with, and I wanted to buy a house and get married and have kids. We worked out a deal where I got $320,000 and a salary bump to $100,000 a year, and I would receive 30 percent of all the income we received from overseas licensing deals. For me, the biggest components of the deal were that my salary was now triple, the company would be financing the acquisition of new masters, and I could focus on production, signing artists, and negotiating overseas deals. And the part of the business I really had no interest in—administration and accounting—would be handled by Rounder. I also retained a 20 percent ownership stake and was still El Presidente. Things with the Rounders got off to a great start. They were in Boston and I was in DC. As long as RAS was making good money they did not really care what I was up to.

I knew I had made it in spite of all the naysayers and nonbelievers who tried to dissuade me from pursing my dreams. I felt empowered. Like Jah had given I and I the strength of a lion. And yes, I could roar.

Mad Professor/Ariwa

I also developed a close relationship with Neil Fraser, a.k.a. the Mad Professor, and his Ariwa (the Yoruba word for *communication*) label out of London, England. I want to emphasize that Neil is perhaps the greatest dub engineer working today, a true visionary cut from the same mold as Lee Perry. His impact cannot be underestimated, and he also is one of the most genuine and considerate people I have ever met. Maximum respect.

Neil and I had a great deal in common: we were close in age, had started our labels around the same time, and it was important to him that the music he produced and released be legitimate and not just a quick hustle. He supported his artists, and Ariwa was like a family. His records were enormously popular on both sides of the pond, and his dub mix of a Massive Attack album for Virgin in 1995 was heralded as one of the great remixes from that time. Born in British Guiana and having lived in England most of his life, Neil also set up a whole complex in Gambia, Africa, and has an annual concert there as well as a studio and home. He really does walk the walk; while many talk about repatriation to Africa, Neil is actually doing it.

Initially RAS released a compilation of what I believed to be some of his most significant tracks, called *It's a Mad, Mad, Mad, Mad Professor*. Soon thereafter we went into a full-blown label deal where RAS would release the entire Ariwa catalog in America, and we were aggressive about releasing and promoting his music here as well. My friendship with Neil remains strong, and he is one person I can count on to do whatever I ask of him, and he knows I'll do the same for him.

Eddy Grant/Ice Records

Around this time I also entered into a working relationship with Eddy Grant's Ice Records from Barbados. As with Ariwa, RAS was the exclusive North American manufacturer and distributor for Ice. Eddy is an amazing artist and a great person with a keen understanding of the karmic reality of life. He had scored a major pop hit with "Electric Avenue," but ended up getting badly ripped off by his business manager in England.

Eddy had a terrific studio in Barbados where the Rolling Stones recorded their album *Voodoo Lounge*. I asked him where the Stones came up with that name, and he explained that he and his wife had over forty cats running around their place, and that Keith Richards had adopted one called Voodoo and ended up naming the album after this little kitten.

Eddy also told me about once being called into a meeting by Chris Blackwell in the middle of the night when Bob Marley was dying in Germany; Chris had the audacity of proposing to launch Eddy as the next dreadlock superstar in reggae music. Eddy had long dreads but was not a devout Rasta. Naturally, Eddy declined Chris's offer and thought it was deceitful that Chris would even make this suggestion while the prophet and true disciple of Jah lay on his deathbed. Many reggae artists have accused Chris of being the devil (including Bunny Wailer and Peter Tosh), and it's perhaps no coincidence that a *Rolling Stone* feature on Chris was titled "A Man of Wealth & Taste"—a line from the Stones song "Sympathy for the Devil."

Live & Learn, *Sky High*, *and Gong Sounds*
I would also try to help other small labels with the manufacturing and distribution of their records. My good friend Barry Wright and I had formed a close connec-

tion from when I would visit his Live & Learn record store on Georgia Avenue in Washington, DC. Barry and I have spent many years reasoning about life, and his label was home to great artists such as Beres Hammond, Dennis Brown, Barrington Levy, Wailing Souls, Mighty Diamonds, Don Carlos, and Junior Reid. He produced a number of excellent recordings and worked closely with his brother Jah Life and famous reggae producer Junjo Lawes. And with a friendship that has endured over thirty years, Barry has taught me the true meaning of the phrase "a brother from another mother." Brethren we are and brethren we shall remain.

Sky High has been closely associated with the Marley family since his time working with Bob Marley. He has taken the Marley youth under his guidance and is often on tour with the various sons and daughters of Bob. Sky and I became acquainted in Jamaica, as he had known Peter Broggs, Bunny Wailer, and many of the artists I worked with once I had established RAS Records. Sky is a heartical brother, also born on His Majesty's birthday, and I always make sure to telephone him on that day. He was the first one to produce a young Luciano and has put out a number of releases of himself singing, under the group name Sky High & the Mau Mau. Sky is the real thing and if you ever buck him up on the road, please make sure to hail him up from I man Doctor Dread.

I also tried to do a thing with Gilly from Gong Sounds. He had been the personal chef to Bob Marley on tour, and he was also respected in Jamaica as a very good footballer. I got to know him when he was working with Bunny Wailer and his Solomonic label. He had opened a nice studio in Miami and produced a number of good tunes, but Gilly would not deal with me straight and our relationship quickly fell apart.

Charlie Chaplin

One of my favorite releases from this period was with Charlie Chaplin. Outside of Yellowman, Tiger, and a few other deejays, RAS was principally a label of singers. Dancehall reggae had not yet taken over and I was more interested in promoting conscious music, yet I liked Charlie's style and his blistering lyrics and wanted to do an LP with him. I went down to Jamaica to discuss the specifics with him and ended up going over to a big concert in Port Antonio where he was performing.

This was just after Hurricane Gilbert had severely torn up Jamaica. I first stopped in Negril, and I remember seeing how in this time of tragedy people came together regardless of how poor they were, and they would help their brothers and sisters in any way they could. And maybe Jah was making it clear that He was actually in control even though mankind believed it could rule this Earth. From there I went to the Eastern Consciousness Music Festival in Port Antonio, which was being held to raise money for the hurricane victims. When I saw how the crowd responded to Charlie Chaplin's live performance, I was blown away. Time and time again the audience would make the band rewind and start back up as they erupted into an uncontrollable frenzy.

My brain shifted gears. I thought about how cool it would be to record a "live" Chaplin album . . . in the studio. We would pick out ten rhythms and invite fifty or sixty of Chaplin's close brethren and mic the crowd. I would bring in cases of Guinness, Red Stripe, lots of weed, food, etc.—the whole deal. Have everyone feeling nice. The Roots Radics would be the backing band and we would just let the twenty-four-track tape run straight through. No stopping. I would also run a two-track tape at the same time. Twenty-five minutes per side. All freestyle. All live. Unrehearsed. When it was time to cut to the next song, the band would just cut. I would call it *Two Sides of Charlie Chaplin*.

This was a completely original idea, one that was consistent with my goal as a producer to capture the true essence of an artist at his or her best. To get that Real Authentic Sound of what it was like to be in a Jamaican dance with the deejay toasting to the delight of the crowd. We booked out Dynamic, as it was the largest studio in Jamaica and I wanted lots of room for Chaplin's brethren. The Rolling Stones and Paul Simon had recorded there and it was an excellent room. The session was phenomenal: The crowd went crazy. The band went crazy. Chaplin went crazy—after the session he and I were outside the studio and he let me pop his .38 into the Kingston night to let off some of my excitement.

This release catapulted Chaplin right to the top of the deejay market, and offers for his live shows came in fast and furious. That night in the studio was fucking electric. And when I think that I was getting paid to do this kind of stuff, I realize once again how truly blessed I am.

Many years later Chaplin came to visit me at my hotel in Kingston. He drove up in his criss BMW SUV and told me how he owed all his success to what I had done for him so many years prior. He now owns a large security company and does a live show on occasion, but just the fact that he was grateful for what I had done goes a long way with me. This is the respect I have talked about receiving in return for what I do for others. It really is such a simple thing. Jah live.

Inner Circle

Another big coup for RAS, although it did not start out that way, was signing Inner Circle, who had become extremely popular in the late '70s. Their lead singer Jacob Miller had a distinctive voice and vocal styling. Hits like "Tenement Yard" became well-known staples in the early days of reggae, but in 1980 Jacob was killed in an automobile crash at the age of twenty-seven. Inner Circle became dormant.

I had become friends with the Lewis brothers, Roger and Ian, who were the principal architects of the group. In their success with Jacob they had migrated to Miami and set up a pressing plant there for the Top Ranking label. They started shipping LPs to me for distribution by the hundreds. One day they told me they had a new lead singer and asked if RAS would be willing to put out their first album as a new group. Inner Circle ended up coming to Washington, DC, and mixed a few tracks, though I was not really involved in any of the production. The album was called *One Way* and we released it to very little fanfare. The response was underwhelming at best.

Out of the blue, the band let me know that this new TV show *Cops* wanted to use the track "Bad Boys" from the album. No one had any idea this TV show and song would blow up so big. And even though most Americans do not know the band Inner Circle, everybody knows

the song "Bad Boys." *Cops* became one of the most popular shows on American television, and the song played
at the beginning and end of each episode. RAS released
a single and it started flying out the door, attracting the
attention of some major labels. We quickly sold well
over a hundred thousand units, but the Lewis brothers
were seasoned veterans of the music business and knew
that to really hit the big time they would need heavy
major label support internationally.

Inner Circle was getting pressure from Warner
Brothers to do a worldwide deal, and Warner Brothers
wanted "Bad Boys" as part of it. Never one to impede
the potential of how far an artist could reach, I agreed
to turn over the rights to the *One Way* album and their
follow-up LP that contained the hit "Sweat."

One of my biggest regrets is that I did not demand
a piece of the publishing rights when Inner Circle first
approached me to put out the *One Way* album. Considering that "Bad Boys" gets played multiple times a night in
every TV market in the US (not counting all its various
other uses), my publishing company would have been
making hundreds of thousands each year just off this
one song. Damn, that sounds like retirement money. I
will say that I am extremely proud of Inner Circle, and
that they took their good fortune and built the nicest studio I have ever set foot in just outside of Miami. Circle
Sounds. We still talk regular and I and I remain brethren.

Tiger
I have mentioned that RAS did not put out many records
with deejays, and that it was mostly singers that made
up our roster. But when I first heard Tiger, I lost my shit

and I still have not found it. Tiger had released a couple of songs in Jamaica that went straight to number one. He was so hot you could not even get near him. Fortunately for me, the local Washington producer Papa Biggs was working with Tiger on all these tracks. He came to me to put out the LP and we both knew it had to be rush-rush-rush. All I can say is that RAS went into hypermode and got that album onto the street as quickly as we could. Fuck release dates and setting it up to promote and sell. This was happening *now*. And this is where an independent label can outmaneuver the majors.

The major labels are like big oil tankers and need time to get their ship to turn. Kind of like the *Titanic*. Independents do whatever we want. We hit the street running. I have never seen twenty thousand copies of an LP fly out the door so fast. It sold like hot bread. Now, when the big labels talk about selling millions and you hear me talking about selling thousands, you must be thinking, *Big deal*. But for an independent label it *is* a big deal. It is a big deal just to be able to pay your employees, pay the artists a fair shake, and keep the doors open and the heat turned on. Ask any owner of an independent label and they will tell you the same.

At the time Exxon gas stations were giving away tiger tails to hang from your rearview mirror, and I talked a gas station owner into selling me two hundred of these so I could send them out with the records to radio deejays and writers. We always tried to include something cool with our releases so the deejays would remember RAS and how we always gave you a little extra. We made yellow condoms for the *Yellowman Rides Again* record. I had one of my employees go to Baltimore and buy some extra-mampi-sized cheap women's underwear which we put around the LP sleeve of Little Lenny's "Gun in a Baggy" (a song that had been banned on Jamaican radio but became a huge smash in the dancehalls where the authorities could not put a stop to it). The song referred to gonorrhea in a woman's baggies (underwear).

When Tiger's LP dropped, I set up a US tour that would feature him at all the important venues across the country, hoping it would help him cross over into the US hip-hop market. Our first show was at SOBs in New York, and Tiger tore up the place. The crowd went wild. The next day we were scheduled to fly out to Chicago when we discovered that Tiger had vanished. Just disappeared. Evidently he went back to Jamaica, and we had to cancel the tour. No reason. No explanation. He was just gone. Many years later while in Kingston I heard on the radio that Tiger had been in a motorcycle accident and had suffered severe brain damage. He never recovered to the point where he could resume his recording career, and I never saw him again after that night at SOBs.

Dancehall Consciousness

Of all the many promotional items I came up with, the one I was most proud of were these miniature brooms made by the Bobo dreads in Jamaica. At this point, Shabba Ranks and dancehall had taken over the Jamaican reggae scene. The music was created on drum machines with little or no melody, and the lyrics often presented misogynistic views toward women or sexual bravado and gangster attitudes extolling the virtues of guns. This was not the vibe or style of the music of Bob Marley and what first brought me into the reggae music business. I made the conscious decision that RAS Records would not support this. Yes, dancehall took over and labels like VP and Greensleeves were there to support it all the way. I sometimes wonder if this was the beginning of reggae's downward spiral; just like hip-hop and rap had gained major traction in the US market, dancehall became the preferred choice of the reggae audience.

While it would be foolish to just sit on the sidelines and not get into the game, at the same time I could not earnestly support something that went against the principles I had established for RAS. I had seen the longevity in artists like Bunny Wailer, Burning Spear, Culture, and Israel Vibration, who all had successful careers for upward of thirty years. Foundation artists. So I decided to release three albums (the Power of the Trinity working yet again) by conscious dancehall artists. I wanted to show the public that dancehall rhythms could be used to convey positive messages and that there were artists who were capable of being more sophisticated in constructing their songs, like Tony Rebel, Angie Angel, and Chaka Demus & Pliers.

I was still close with Junior Reid from his days as lead singer with Black Uhuru and I knew he was tight with the Bobo dread sect in Jamaica. I had seen the Bobos in and around Kingston selling brooms they made from raw materials they gathered in the bush, and I asked Reid if he could get them to make three hundred hand-sized brooms for me to promote a campaign I wanted to launch called *Clean up the Dancehall*.

Reid took care of this for me and I sent out the three releases to all the deejays and writers with the broom included, along with a letter about how it was time to clean up the dancehall and help elevate the consciousness of the people while still being current with the new beats they were looking for. It caused quite a controversy. But I like controversy. It makes people think and communicate with each other.

I came to find out that Jamaican Prime Minister Michael Manley had used the broom and its symbolic implications to convey his message of cleaning up Jamaica during one of his campaigns. At one point, even the owners of VP Records called me to ask what I was up to—but in the end my efforts never really amounted to much. The people wanted slackness, and RAS fell back in the race. I knew I couldn't compete if I had to sacrifice my integrity for the potential of monetary gains.

Tenor Saw

Whenever I heard a new artist with a completely unique style I would do my best to find this person and get him or her to record for RAS. In the case of Tenor Saw it was an obsession that started when I first heard his singular vocal stylings. I was completely blown away. He had released a few singles and all of Jamaica was up in arms about this exciting new talent. Plus, I thought his name was really cool.

When I inquired as to where Tenor Saw lived I was told he resided in a ghetto of Kingston known as Painland. So I drove in there, parked my car, and started to ask people where Saw lived. Some tough-looking youths came up to me, and I could see their bodies had been burned by acid; this was a common form of retribution in those times in Kingston. It was a rough place for a white man to be walking through, and after letting off some small money, the youths explained to me that Tenor Saw was not home at the time. I decided it would be best to return to my car and leave that place without creating too much of a disturbance. When I later told some people I had gone into Painland to look for Tenor Saw, they were shocked and explained that it was one of the most dangerous parts of the city.

A short time later his first LP was released with Sugar Minott as the producer on Lloyd Evans's Blue Mountain label. So I just let it go. But several years later I finally made contact with Tenor Saw. By this time he had moved to New York and word on the street was that he had gotten mixed up with drugs and was not behaving in a normal manner.

I arranged to have him come to Washington, DC, to voice a few tunes for me with the intention of producing a full album. When we started running the twenty-four-track tape in the studio, Saw would just repeat the same lines over and over again. I suggested that he turn the song into a full story, and I even gave him some lyrics and ideas, but every time we hit the record button he would just keep repeating the same lines. After three different rhythms I decided to give up on the idea and see if we could regroup at a later time; I offered him a copy of the rhythms so he could work on the lyrics back in New York. He stepped into the control room completely overcome with paranoia and told me that I had recorded his voice onto the twenty-four-track tape, that I was going to keep it and rip him off. If was the first and only time I had to take out a razor knife and cut off all the recording tape.

I drove Saw back to his hotel and gave him some train fare to return to New York and told him everything was all right. By this time his paranoia had grown so intensely that it made me really uncomfortable just to be sitting with him in the car. I tried to assure him everything was okay and that the sun would rise again tomorrow. He responded by telling me the last person who had said that to him had tried to kill him. He pulled up his pant leg and showed me a scar where a bullet still remained. I realized then and there that Tenor Saw was mentally ill and that nothing I could say would calm him down. It was scary, sad, and confusing. His brain was out of control.

Two weeks later he was found dead on the streets of Houston, a victim of a crack cocaine overdose; it was a depressing ending for one of the great Jamaican artists of his time. His music still endures and eventually I was given the rights by Lloyd at Blue Mountain to release some of his music on RAS.

Rastafari Elders

Another CD that is particularly meaningful to me is the one I produced with the Rastafari Elders. Jake Homiak from the Smithsonian Institution had brought a number of elder Rastafari to Washington, DC, to participate in the annual Folklife Festival on the National Mall. Jake had spent much time in Jamaica documenting the livity of Rastafari, and my idea was to have each of the seven Elders speak into the microphone and explain in their own words the meaning of Rastafari. To release the seven seals thereof.

Marcus Garvey, the Jamaican-born pan-Africanist

who advocated the repatriation of blacks to Africa, had told that a black king descended from Solomon and King David would be born in Africa as the Messiah, the Second Coming of Christ. And when His Imperial Majesty Emperor Haile Selassie I the First (a direct descendant to King David and Solomon) was crowned emperor of Ethiopia, this fulfillment of prophecy had now presented itself. (There are many books on Marcus Garvey, Haile Selassie, and Rastafari that explore these tenets more deeply.) On the recording of the Elders, between each oration there would be traditional chanting and drumming with percussion that were common at Rastafari gatherings, or groundations, in Jamaica.

I felt like Moses Asch from Folkways Records. The entire CD was recorded at Lion and Fox in the dark of the night. A single night. I cannot describe how I felt when I emerged from the studio into the morning light. I knew something remarkable had taken place and that its significance would exist for-iver. This was the ancient wisdom of the Rastafari which has no beginning and can never have an end. In addition to the recording itself, the naturalness of the CD cover (designed by the incomparable Mitch "Ites" Goldberg with beautiful photography from Peter Barry) and the liner notes by a Rasta in DC named Farika made the album come together perfectly. Even today, universities across the world use this album to teach classes about Rastafari—and I and I praise Jah for having been involved in the creation of this seminal release.

Joseph Hill/Culture

I could not write about RAS Records without including these words about my dear friend and brother Joseph Hill of Culture. One of the most creative minds and down-to-earth people I have ever met, Joseph literally worked himself to death and finally succumbed while on tour in Germany in 2006. Joe and I had a closeness that is hard to describe. He saw the world and life much differently from most people, and was able to articulate these sentiments in the music he wrote. His popularity in Jamaica and within reggae circles around the world was enormous, thanks to anthems like "International Herb." His prophetic song "Two Sevens Clash" inspired the name taken by rock legends the Clash.

Though I had known Joseph casually for a long time, our relationship was cemented after the Israeli reggae producer Guil Bonstein (who also owned a cool reggae club in Tel Aviv where all the top Jamaican acts would play) was down in Jamaica producing a new Culture record, and he ended up asking if RAS wanted to release it. I spent a memorable week in the studio mixing the album in DC with Guil, Joseph, and Jim Fox; the *Good Things* CD was my first Culture release, and included many wicked dubs provided by Jim. Culture and I moved from strength to strength and although I was never responsible for producing any of the albums, RAS became his home for many years.

Joseph once related to me a backstage incident in Europe where Quincy Jones told him how much he had loved his show, and how Quincy had always wanted to produce a reggae artist of his caliber. He gave Joseph all his phone numbers and told him that he was ready to work with him anytime, anyplace. Joseph told his wife Pauline that he preferred to "stay with the evil I and I already know"—namely, Doctor Dread. I'm not sure if I should have taken this as a compliment, and I respect that Joseph chose me over the great Quincy Jones, but the point is that he was a loyal soldier. That is just how he trod.

We continued with *One Stone*, which was an enormous hit record all around the world, especially in Europe and South Africa. Again Mitch "Ites" Goldberg did a stunning cover, thanks to an exceptional photo taken by Brian Jahn of Joseph holding a large crystal under a waterfall outside of Kingston. For me, it was the best of all the Culture CDs that RAS released, and its sales were so spectacular that we were able to advance Joseph $75,000 for his next record and an additional $50,000 for the publishing rights.

This was the most RAS had ever paid for a release, but I felt so good about giving this kind of money to Joe. With it, he was able to complete the construction of his house. He also built a studio. It just put him on solid ground. I came out to his house in the hills just above Kingston and I am not sure which of us was prouder. We sat on his veranda that day and drank and smoked with all his family and I knew that Jah was great and together we were His blessed servants. I miss Joseph so much that I often talk to him even though he is no longer here among us. See you around, my friend.

Augustus Pablo and Hugh Mundell

I was also close with Augustus Pablo, who released several of his CDs with us and overdubbed melodica on numerous RAS productions, including our first Israel Vibration album, *Strength of My Life*. He would come to the studio with a very large bag of weed, his suru board (a wood plank used for cutting weed), and his coconut chalice. There would always be an enormous cloud of ganja smoke when Pablo came in to work. Of course, the *No Smoking* signs in the studio were completely ignored. The chalice is a serious thing and Pablo would hit it hard.

RAS also licensed the classic Hugh Mundell *Africa Must Be Free* LP. This was a remarkable and inspirational Augustus Pablo production with a young artist, and it was loved by reggae fans the world over. It was another great milestone for RAS and a tremendous honor for me personally. Jamaican artists were among the first to sing out against apartheid in South Africa, and the title track directly addressed this topic and also preached of African unity. In fact, Jamaica was one of the first places Nelson Mandela traveled to after his release from prison in 1990, a testament to the country's firm and consistent stance against apartheid. This album showed Pablo at his best musically, and this young new artist had a vocal style and vibe that really encompassed the spirit of Rastafari.

Several years later I met with Hugh Mundell while I was working at Tuff Gong studios in Kingston, and we agreed on a deal with RAS and everything was set. The very next day he was shot and killed while driving in a car with his brother, who had gotten mixed up in a robbery. It was incredibly sad to see such a young, promising talent gone before he could even begin to reach his full potential. Pablo also left us at a young age, despite the best efforts of his close friend Dera Tompkins at the NIH's National Library of Medicine in DC, who treated the infection that eventually overcame his body.

The Marleys

When Cedella Marley and the Tuff Gong label approached me to release a Bob Marley interview CD, I was very moved. Bob Marley on RAS Records. And even though it was an interview album with pieces of his music intertwined, it was still amazing to have been chosen to put this out. They say that many are called but few are chosen.

I had known the Marley family for a while and my long history of working with Tuff Gong in Jamaica was rewarded with this release. I also began to promote some shows with Stephen Marley when he was getting ready to release his first CD. His booking agent asked me to arrange a concert at a Jamaican venue in DC, so I set up a gig at Crossroads with the Mad Professor opening.

In his earlier performances there was a shyness to Stephen that some people may have thought of as discomfort over performing live onstage. But he impressed me as just a humble youth. I remember bumping fists with his young son Jeremiah in the back of the tour bus, and I just said the word "Rasta." Jeremiah looked up at his dad and said, "That man just said *Rasta*," and Steve simply nodded his head. I had been sold on both Steve and his brother Damian from when they produced *Chant Down Babylon*, a CD of rap artists mixed onto Bob Marley songs with new beats they laid down and mixed in with the original tracks. Yes, they were born with the name Marley and were offspring of the great Bob, but this CD showed how they were two studio wizards who took their music very seriously, and I was blown away by what they created, regardless of their name.

I produced more shows with Steve and Damian in Washington, DC, and made a personal commitment within I-self to always be there for them and do the best job I could in advancing their careers. Not that they needed me, but it was a vibe I carried with me in all my dealings with them. Later, when Bunny Wailer was asked to be part of the Roots Rock Reggae tour with Steve and Ziggy, and I was on the tour in the capacity of Bunny's manager, our relationship was further strengthened. After the last gig in DC, we had a big party at my house to celebrate the success of the tour. When Steve was walking through my garage I pointed out my vintage Rolls Royce station wagon and asked him if he knew what the RR on the hubcaps stood for. He looked at me and without skipping a beat said, "RAS Records." He knew from his dad's BMW that those initials stood for Bob Marley and the Wailers, so he figured out the RR on mine.

Over time Steve grew much more comfortable performing onstage and his first solo CD release was very well received. I did a sold-out show with Steve and Damian just after *Welcome to Jamrock* had exploded. On the tour bus after the show I thanked them both and told them I had made a lot of money that night. They were glad to hear this and Damian said, "How you mean?" which is the Jamaican way of saying, *Of course you did.* And when Damian and rapper Nas came through town I again promoted the show and the energy in the 9:30 Club that night made the roof blow off the place. My good friends Seth Hurwitz and Rich Heinecke who own the club would always give me the first shot at producing reggae shows there, and it was an extremely generous gesture to turn this one over to me, since it was an obvious sellout and probably the highest grossing concert I ever did as a promoter.

Damian was being interviewed on his bus after the show, and between interviews I asked him about his lyrics in a song he did with Nas, "Road to Zion": *"A two gun me have, me bust dem inna stereo."* I thought those were wicked lyrics and asked him if he took them from a Western novel or movie and he said, "No man, original." And when I asked him how he wrote such an amazing song as "Welcome to Jamrock," he explained that he had just written a single verse for a mash-up (where many artists all contribute one or two verses on a rhythm for a street mixtape), but when people began telling him how killer it was he sat down a few months later and composed the entire song over the course of the next few days. Now that is talent. You dig?

And during the most recent solo show Steve did for me at the 9:30 Club, there was a natural mystic in the air. Steve was channeling the spirit of Bob and I felt he was not looking for commercial success but instead had chosen to continue the real work of his father. Damian was doing a more deejay style of hip-hop reggae and Ziggy had a more traditional reggae sound, but in Steve I felt the actual presence of Bob. And the crowd felt it as well that night. He was confident and it just flowed through him. I and I know there is much great work left to come from all the Marley youth and I look forward to seeing and hearing what is in store for us all.

EARLY LIFE

Once a man and twice a child. And everything is just for a while.
—Bob Marley, from the song "Real Situation"

I was born Gary Himelfarb on December 2, 1954, at George Washington University Hospital in Washington, DC, the same day Joseph McCarthy was censured for interrogating people's affiliation with the Communist Party. Like many white Jewish families we moved out to the suburbs when I was in first grade. I had a good childhood. I was into sports, had lots of friends, and did well in school. I know Sigmund Freud says that many of our childhood experiences will affect how we turn out later in life, and I think to some degree this is true. I remember as a ten-year-old I had this little battery-powered record player, and I would take it to our neighborhood swimming pool along with my little red box full of 45 rpm records and play them for all my friends. I was the president of the chorus in junior high school and would lead warmups and learned about song arrangements from my teacher Miss Kerr. Don't let 'em fool you: good teachers who can inspire the youth are worth their weight in gold. I believe this led me into becoming a record producer.

When I entered high school I was still into sports and went out for the junior varsity football team. I could catch a football like no one else and was dubbed "Hands Himelfarb." For me this was what it was all about. Playing football. Making friends. The cheerleaders. I was doing pretty good at practice, but after a scrimmage one day I was horsing around on the bus ride home with the rest of the team and for some strange reason the coach cut me. Just like that. I was devastated. One week later I was at this big field party near my house and all these hippies were smoking weed and probably doing psychedelics (this was 1969) and I entered a world I had never been to before. I was completely transformed from jock to hippie, and to this day my mom says that her biggest regret in life, as far as I am concerned, is that she did not go back to the coach and demand that I get reinstated to the team.

Drugs soon became a very important part of my life. I would smoke weed at seven thirty a.m. before school with friends on the railroad tracks. I also experimented with psychedelics (in particular LSD). My first airplane ride was to visit some distant relatives living in Cleveland so I could see a Salvador Dalí exhibition. I had brought some LSD to take with me and I dropped just prior to entering the museum. The Dalí canvases were fantastic. Large, surrealistic landscapes including one called *The Hallucinogenic Toreador*. Believe me, the LSD took me deep into these landscapes, and when recounting this story at a recent dinner party I joked that I have never returned from these adventures down that rabbit hole. For some reason everyone at the table thought I was serious!

Our parents did not understand the drug culture and were unprepared to cope with it. When I told them in high school each night that I was going to the library to study (even though I had hair down to my shoulders and a flowered headband on and was wasted 24/7), they somehow believed me. Now that is fucking funny! One time I came home completely wasted when my parents were entertaining some friends, and they were of course horrified by my condition. They asked their friends to leave, then made me drink three or four glasses of straight gin. They said, "So how are you feeling now?" and I answered that I was actually feeling even better than when I got home. Looking back on it now, I actually feel bad for what my parents had to endure, as they were totally unequipped to deal with the generational shift which had taken place in the '60s. Fortunately, I came through these years pretty much unscathed and have had a great relationship with my parents ever since. My dad passed away about ten years ago but I still speak with my mom almost every day.

I managed to get through high school and graduate but never did make it to a single day of college. Though I do want much better for my kids. I believe that it is important to provide a brighter future for my children and give them the tools they need to be successful. I have exposed them to many peoples and cultures around the world, and have always taught them that hard work and moderation are the keys to a sane and productive life. I pray for them and encourage them to not take the same path as their dad. And I show them love. That's all I can do. It's up to them to do the rest.

THIS BUSINESS CALLED MUSIC

The music business is a cruel and shallow money trench,
a long plastic hallway where thieves and pimps run free,
and good men die like dogs.
—Creatively adapted from a quote
by Hunter S. Thompson

I n 1990 my first son was born. Parents often listen to nursery rhymes from people like Raffi and watch big purple dinosaurs on TV with their kids. My wife and I thought about how soothing and contemporary a *Reggae for Kids* album would be. Songs with positive messages for children that both they and their parents could enjoy listening to with that nice relaxing reggae beat. I moved forward with this concept and decided to add a number of baby boomer songs from my childhood like "Puff the Magic Dragon" and "Somewhere Over the Rainbow." We were not seeing dollar signs and thinking about how much money this would generate, yet it became the biggest and most profitable release in RAS Records history. It originated from a place of love. Love for our newborn baby and the blessings that come with children.

I picked out the songs and then thought about which artists could perform them, and helped write some lyrics to impart the positive messages. It was a joy creating this album, and I learned that when you do something from pure love, you may be blessed with the greatest amount of money you could ever imagine. I have always believed that when you do good that good will come back to you—and this has been an important aspect of how I live my life.

RAS earned profits of over a million dollars from this release. It was licensed all around the world with the jackets printed in many different languages. I got letters from teachers of autistic children who told me that this was the only thing that could calm down their class and bring them serenity. It became so popular in Jamaica that a radio show called *Reggae for Kids* came on each morning at six thirty a.m. on Irie FM when everyone was getting ready for school and work, and its theme song was taken from our album. And twenty years later the show is still on every morning and people all over the island start their day with a positive message and some irie vibes. You see how Jah works? My goal of spreading the positive vibes and sounds of reggae internationally was becoming a reality. Once again, we had incredible packaging, which had become our forte, courtesy of another warm, spiritual, and positive cover from Mitch "Ites" Goldberg.

I followed this up with *More Reggae for Kids*, and then my European distributor suggested that I do a *Reggae for Kids* with all Disney songs. The first two *Reggae for Kids* releases had both been huge successes, and I figured that since everyone knew and loved the songs from Disney, this should be even bigger and could cross over into more homes outside of the reggae market. Of course, the release had to be relevant to Jamaican culture, and I still had to live up to the Real Authentic Sound I had promised. In my head I heard Bunny Wailer doing "Hakuna Matata" from *The Lion King*. Tony Rebel doing "Bare Necessities" from *The Jungle Book*. Even Gregory Isaacs doing "When I See an Elephant Fly" from *Dumbo*.

The recordings were amazing. People were blown away by reggae renditions of these Disney classics. My friend John Simson sent out the master to people he knew at Disney to see if they would be interested in licensing the CD for the Disney label, and they loved it. They offered me a $75,000 advance and said that they would feature it on the Disney TV channel, and do a special promotion for it at Disney World featuring artists from Jamaica. That they would create animated videos for the project and that the CD cover art would be complete with all the Disney characters. The project would reek of Disney. In addition, they would hire me to be the executive producer of a whole series of Disney collections such as *Disney Blues, Disney Jazz, Disney Goes Latin*, and so on. I could see myself entering a whole new echelon of the music business. Hanging out with Disney executives and flying out to LA and having astronomical production budgets—visions of grandeur.

But people close to me talked me out of it. My US distributor projected that I would get at least $500,000 in profits from them based on the sales of the previous two *Reggae for Kids* albums, which made the Disney advance look small. My overseas partners were also pushing for me not to give it to Disney, as it would then fall out of their distribution. And then a good friend from LA who worked in the film industry told me that Disney was a big corporate motherfucker, and that all the people he knew who had worked on the *Cool Runnings* film, a Disney production, felt that they had gotten ripped off. I had heard similar things about Disney and knew there were books written about what a big evil empire they had become.

So the independent rebel in me turned them down and I decided to put it out on my own in 2001. Disney warned me not to use any of their characters in the artwork and that I could not use the Disney name in the title. And although the CD turned out to do very well, it was not the success I had hoped it would be. By this time the music industry had started to collapse with the advent of Napster and other free downloading sites. And my US distributor that had promised me big bucks actually ended up filing for bankruptcy and burned me for over $300,000. Other than the "Bad Boys" publishing oversight, this was the biggest mistake of my career in the music business. Who knows what Jah would have had in store for me if I had gone along with the Mouse down that yellow brick road?

With the exception of very early agreements with Freddie McGregor and Black Uhuru, RAS always did one-album deals with artists. I did not want to sign the artists for long-term deals, as their ancestors had already borne the brunt of slavery, and I always felt the music industry created long-term contracts in a contemporary effort to own slaves. The labels would claim to be protecting their investments but it was more about denying the artists the freedom they deserved. I told the artists that we could do an album together, and if we were both satisfied with the experience they could come back and do another one. That way they were free to go elsewhere if they were not pleased with how RAS had treated them. And at the same time I wanted to educate the artists about what is a very complicated business. To empower them with knowledge so they could navigate through the treacherous minefields where record labels, music publishers, booking agents, and managers were all looking to get a piece of what they had created. I always took the time to try to fully explain, to the best of my ability, all of the nuances that could have an effect on their careers.

Sometimes I would lose artists this way, as they would get higher offers from larger labels, but for the most part our return rate was excellent. And I liked that the artists knew they were free, and that this might inspire them to produce their best possible music for me. If an artist was miserable with his label, what would stop him from going to the studio and wasting a bunch of money to turn out some worthless crap just to show his discontent? (This is why I often suggest that everyone in the industry should read the manifesto *The Business of Music*.) I always felt really good about sending artists checks and paying them their royalties. I knew life was not easy for most of them, and I was glad to get them some money, especially after seeing how other labels (especially the majors) dealt with them. If RAS made a video or some cool item to help promote their albums we never charged them back for this. Even if we gave artists tour support (and we often did), this was never recouped from their royalties.

That word "recoup" has some very interesting implications in the major leagues, as I would later learn in my dealings with Sanctuary Records. *Everything* got recouped. It was in the contract. It was the norm for major labels to squeeze out as much as they could for themselves, which is why there is often such an adversarial relationship between artists, managers, lawyers, and the labels. Almost an us-against-them mentality. Chaka Demus & Pliers once told me that after having three songs hit the Top Ten of the British pop charts, Island Records sent a royalty statement showing they still had an "unrecouped" royalty balance of close to 100,000 pounds. Sure, they had made expensive music videos and went to England to perform on *Top of the Pops*, but they had no clue that all these expenses were coming out of their own pockets. Why should the label care if the video director showed up in a limo? Or if the catering on the set was first class? The artist was paying for it anyway.

RAS did not operate that way. Usually it was my station wagon that went to the airport to pick up the artists, and my home became known as Hotel Himelfarb to the musicians staying there so we could save on expenses in order to put out the best music possible. Spending money in the studio was my highest budgetary priority.

My good friend Marc Appelbaum, who owned the thirty-five-store chain Kemp Mill Records in Washington, DC, told me he never understood the excesses of the music industry. He explained how Sony would spend

$30,000 on a luncheon in New York with fancy food at some expensive restaurant and bring in artists like Celine Dion to impress all the big record store owners, and the label would pay for all the retailers' hotels and travel. Wine and dine them to the max. I was once at a Christmas party held at the Kemp Mill warehouse and I noticed a few skids of Prince CDs stacked way up in the air. I asked someone what they were doing up there and they told me that the label had asked them to make a "political buy" to make it look like the Prince release was number one on the *Billboard* charts. They would be able to return these for full credit in two months, before payment was due on them. All smoke and mirrors. No wonder Prince stuck his middle finger in the air and waved it at the big corporate labels.

I still say it was the major record companies that killed the music business and not illegal downloading. If a CD could retail for ten dollars, you would have a consumer who would support the music business and the artists instead of opting out to download music for free. What was the purpose for selling a Britney Spears CD for $18.99 when it only cost the label seventy-five cents to manufacture it? Again, the answer is simple: greed. The major labels could not control their greed. Greed in keeping as much money from the artists as possible, and greed in soaking the consumer for way more than they were prepared to spend. And this doesn't even scratch the surface of the horror stories of other backdoor deals and how "payola" dictated what was played on the radio.

In the 1980s and '90s, there had been a great prolifer-

ation of big-box record stores like Virgin, HMV, and
Tower. Both Best Buy and Circuit City also expanded
their CD selections, so there was a much larger distribution pipeline to fill. The problem was that in the music
business you sell the product to a distributor, who in
turn resells it to the music stores, and it is all 100 percent returnable. Anything that doesn't sell comes back to
the label, and this larger pipeline meant larger returns.
Instead of getting monthly checks from our distributors,
so much product would be returned that we got "upside
down" with them and they were instead asking us for
big checks to balance out the accounts. This meant that
we had thousands of CDs in our warehouse with no one
to sell them to, and the money we thought we had in the
bank had to be repaid to our distributors. This effectively
led to a situation where the labels financed the entire
record industry, since we paid for everything from the
manufacturing to artist royalties to returns.

We were not alone. All the other labels were feeling
the same pinch and Rounder, our owner at that stage,
did not blame RAS for this unfortunate financial cir-
cumstance. But they did start to tighten the screws. If
I wanted to spend even five hundred dollars, they required an explanation of what I was spending it on and
whether it was really necessary. Cost-cutting was the
order of the day, and the freedom I had felt in running
RAS had been taken away from me by CFOs in Boston
who were watching every dime. It wasn't the kind of
situation I was comfortable with and I soon told the
Rounders I was coming to Boston to discuss our future
relationship.

I have been told that while many people see the

world in numbers, I see it in colors. Some might say I take an unorthodox approach to life and money, but that is just me. I told the Rounders that day that I was leaving the company and they could sort out my 20 percent ownership sometime down the road. I was moving on. They tried to discourage me and said we could work everything out, and that a RAS without Doctor Dread at the helm was like a ship lost at sea, but I stood firm.

Later that evening Bill Nowlin suggested that instead of leaving I could just buy out their 80 percent stake. I had never thought of that but it sounded like a pretty interesting idea. And thanks to my lawyer Rich Bar and his insistence that I set a goal and then together we figure out how to get to the finish line, I ultimately found a way to buy back their 80 percent stake in RAS, and in 1997 I was once again the *soul* owner of the company.

RAS occupied a small suite of offices on the second floor of a building in Silver Spring, Maryland. Tafari Music also had its offices there, and it was nice to have RAS and Tafari reunited. We were trodding along again and continued to release a steady stream of music. Our relationships with our overseas distributors were still intact and we were able to survive. But in 2001 a confluence of events put the company in a precarious position. Our distributor, Valley Music, one of the largest record distributors in the world, filed for bankruptcy. The owner Barney Cohen, who had become a friend along the way, took his company public and raised loads of money (I even got in on the IPO before realizing that the whole system felt dirty, so I got out)—and then, *boom*, it all fell apart. Valley Music went bankrupt and shares in the company became worthless. Because US bankruptcy laws protect the rich and fuck the less fortunate, I ended up having to buy back the inventory that I owned, and this whole affair set me back $300,000. It was a lot to swallow.

This was around the same time that Napster set up shop on the Internet and people now had the ability to download music for free, which signaled the beginning of the end for the music industry as we knew it. Throughout history, from Edison cylinders to 78s and LPs, from eight-track tapes and cassettes to eventually CDs, it was the record companies who told you how you were going to buy your music. But the paradigm had shifted. The consumer was now telling the record labels how they wanted to get their music. Yet the labels did not want to abdicate this power to the consumer. They wanted the control. The writing was on the wall but the record companies refused to see it. Instead of trying to make a deal with companies like Napster, the greedy motherfuckers decided to sue college kids and their moms instead. If the majors could have seen the forest through the trees and offered the two college kids who started Napster something like $500 million to become partners and figure out a way to monetize the new file-sharing phenomena, then maybe the music industry would not have collapsed. The consumer was rebelling.

Record labels were now thought of as big evil corporate rip-offs, and the consumer had no remorse in stealing music from the web. Even some recording artists started bypassing labels and using the Internet to connect directly with their audience. Many other free download sites popped up, and piracy became rampant. Out of control. It brought the music industry to its knees. I knew it was just a matter of time before all of this would implode and the music industry would be a shambles.

My good friend Don Rose who had founded Ryko-disc, at one time the largest independent record label in America, suggested I contact Sanctuary Records about buying RAS. Sanctuary had just bought Trojan Records, which held the most significant catalog of reggae music (outside of Studio One and Island) from the early '60s through the late '70s. By adding the RAS repertoire they could arguably own the most important reggae over a span of almost three decades. Sanctuary said they were definitely interested in making the acquisition. At the same time, my friend and lawyer Rich Bar was carving out an employment contract for me that would ensure me a good salary for the next three to four years. During the negotiations, I had to sell our house in Jamaica so we could continue to pay our bills at RAS. The clock was ticking and I could feel the whole music industry con-tracting as record stores began to close left and right.

RAS had shown losses of over $100,000 and $200,000 for the previous two years and we were struggling to hang on. Some people told me that I was fooling my-self and that Sanctuary would never buy a company that was losing money, but I still believed it made sense be-cause of the value of the catalog. Nicole and Liz at RAS were putting together the figures Sanctuary requested for their due diligence. But things were taking way too long. Ultimately, around thirteen months passed before we signed a deal. I had now sold my company twice and was ready to move into a new phase of my music career. Of course, I had to first get artists who had originally made handshake deals with RAS to sign actual contracts, which was a tough job but was made easier by the goodwill we had generated over the years.

I was visiting my mother in Florida the day the wire for a little bit under one million dollars from Sanctuary hit my account. Man, did that feel good. I had lots of bills to pay off with that money, and while there was not much left for me after it was all said and done, I still had a high-paying job in the reggae music business and had managed to hold onto my publishing company. But for that moment I had a million dollars in the bank and as I looked out over the ocean and into the horizon, I again knew it was Jah who was blessing me, and I was so thankful that I do not remember if I laughed or cried. But I do know I gave thanks with all of my spirit.

Things at Sanctuary were interesting, to say the least. It was the first time I had worked for what was essentially a major label. We were distributed by Warner Bros. and then Sony/BMG, and there was certainly a pervasive corporate attitude within the company. Many years before I had been part of an independent label organization known as NAIRD (National Association of Independent Record Distributors). I made quite a few friends there and learned the ins and outs of the music industry. Collectively the independents had a bigger share than any one of the individual five major labels so we were definitely a force to be reckoned with. I was voted by my peers to serve on the board of directors one year, which was a great honor. To know that my fellow independent label owners respected me enough to have me represent them was a good feeling. But that camaraderie had faded into a distant memory as NAIRD dissolved with much of the rest of the music industry. Now I was with Sanctuary. Budgets. Sales projections. Egos. I had been told by someone working there that it was impossible to get fired and that the company did not know its head from its tail.

Admittedly, I had the opportunity to produce some great records while I was there, including the Bob Dylan reggae tribute CD. We also signed and released CDs by Steel Pulse and Sizzla. And an amazing CD from Nasio called *Living in the Positive*. Steel Pulse was one of my all-time favorite groups, and this led to me growing close with their lead singer David Hinds, who along with Sly Dunbar and Gregory Isaacs is one of the true geniuses I have met in the reggae business. I could tell from his songwriting, with its melodic and lyrical sophistication, that this was no ordinary person. The album *African Holocaust* is one of the best CDs we ever released. Every song a stunner.

So in many ways my years at Sanctuary were quite positive. I had an expense budget that covered my travel and entertainment costs. Excess spending was the order of the day, and I was told that if I did not spend this money allocated to me for travel and entertainment each year that I would be in danger of having it reduced. Excellent restaurants, nice hotels, traveling first class. Just turn in the receipts and a check would be mailed to you. Paris is my favorite city in the world and the company sent me there once a year to stimulate my creative energy. I visited our main offices in London once a year too. And the more trips I took to Jamaica, the better.

Life was good. No, life was great. It's almost embarrassing how much I was getting paid, along with all the additional benefits being heaped on me. But you know what happens to a house of cards: eventually it collapses. And Sanctuary was hemorrhaging money at a time when the music industry continued to shrink. As Tower Records and HMV shuttered their stores, Sanctuary went into panic mode. It seemed like every week in *Billboard* there were reports of how much money the company was losing, and how the bank was calling in their loans. Before long, we could all see the company was in free fall.

Then things came to a standstill. No more productions. I was told to just sit tight and wait to see if the company could get itself out of this mess. The trade publications reported the company was over forty million dollars in debt, and that bankruptcy was looming. I continued to get paid and hung in there doing nothing. I felt isolated being in Washington, DC, while everyone else was at our New York and Raleigh offices. This went on for close to one year. And then in 2007, Universal Records swooped in and actually bought the company and all of its debt as well. I tried to buy back the RAS label before the sale went through, but couldn't afford the $1.2 million asking price.

No breaks for Doctor Dread this time. On one hand I felt bad knowing that RAS and I would not be together. I had raised this baby from birth, and the separation anxiety kicked in pretty hard. But on the other hand I felt good that a company that was seemingly as financially secure as Universal now owned the masters, and that the artists should be able to get their royalty statements and payments. Boy, was I wrong.

For most artists it has been a nightmare, and it seems that there is not much interest on the part of Universal to take care of them. I soon started a small label, Tafari Records, and released a few CDs, but I could still see that the music industry was ending for me.

Fortunately, before I resolved to completely leave the game I managed to put together a deal to sell the Greensleeves label and publishing division to Steve Weltman. I had met Steve when he managed Nasio, who I had signed to RAS during my tenure with Sanctuary. Steve was a longtime music veteran and had worked with the Beatles and Chrysalis, among others. He had some venture capital people in Switzerland who made loads of money in the hedge-fund game and wanted to finance the purchase of music labels and music publishing companies. Greensleeves was the top reggae label in England—they had an extensive catalog and were at the forefront of the Jamaican dancehall movement. I had worked with Greensleeves for over twenty years, and became good friends with one of the owners, Chris Sedgwick. Their A&R person and co-owner Chris Cracknell was instrumental in identifying and signing new talent.

I always found it interesting that in the twenty-plus years they owned Greensleeves, Chris Sedgwick had never visited Jamaica and Chris Cracknell had only been there once. Cracknell wasn't really a producer, instead choosing to license music from other producers, and thus rarely worked directly with the actual artists. In this regard RAS and Greensleeves were very different companies—yet we worked together to distribute each other's records, license product for manufacturing, and we were reciprocal publishers of each other's catalogs in our respective territories. Tafari Music collected for Greensleeves Publishing in the US, and Greensleeves collected for us in the UK.

We had some fruitful years together and scored a big hit with the Diwali rhythm from Steven "Lenky" Marsden, which was voiced-over by Sean Paul ("Get Busy"), Wayne Wonder ("No Letting Go"), and Lumidee ("Never Leave You"). All three of these songs crossed over to the pop charts and Tafari collected 50 percent of the proceeds. "Get Busy" spent six weeks at number one on the US pop charts—we collected over a million dollars for that song alone. I remember going to the post office one morning and finding the ASCAP check for radio play and other performances waiting there. I said a prayer over the envelope before I opened it, and lo and behold there was a check in there for nearly $225,000! That remains the single biggest check Tafari Music ever saw. Even after paying Greensleeves and Lenky their respective shares, everybody was able to eat well from this money. I remember thanking Sean Paul backstage at a reggae festival in Paris for paying for my son's college education. He said it was his pleasure and we thumped fists and laughed.

Because of our mutual respect, when Chris told me he was looking to sell the label and publishing company, I was immediately interested in buying it. And although I wasn't able to come up with the financing myself, I brokered the introduction between Greensleeves and Steve Weltman. As my commission for securing the deal, Greensleeves ended up wiring me a whopping $178,500. Considering I was out of work and dealing with serious health issues at the time, this was a blessing. To this day I have the utmost respect for Chris and what he did; although we have not talked in years I can say he is a man of his word. I unfortunately can't say the same for Steve Weltman, who reneged on paying his share of my commission. But I know that Jah always provides and to this day I and I continue to run Tafari Music while Weltman and his investment group had to sell off Greensleeves to VP. And I do not "pity the fool."

Although the record industry is just a skeleton of its former self, music will always be created and heard, and that connection between the artist and fan will always remain. Thank you, Jah, and thank you to all the good and bad people I met along the way who allowed me to have a life of such great fulfillment. Raspect!

My good friend Tom Terrell took this shot when Bob Marley was in Washington, DC, for a record release gathering for the *Survival* LP. Bob signed a bunch of stuff for me and I had a few moments of his time to discuss my radio program and what I was doing for reggae. His whole spirit filled that room with an energy I have only felt one other time—when Nelson Mandela was released from prison and came to speak in Washington.

Giuseppe Franconi

Here's a photo of my mom and dad at a swanky club in New York City. My mom was pregnant with me in her belly. Does this mean it is technically the first photo ever taken of I and I?

Joshua Rabinowitz

This was taken at summer camp and most people cannot pick me out. I'm the dark-skinned boy wearing the flowered shirt. To this day people are always asking me what country I am from and I do not feel obliged to answer as I am from the world.

Doctor Dread as he entered high school. I had that clean-cut American look, had been brought up in the suburbs of Washington, DC, and was into sports, girls, and studying hard.

Bill Collins

Stuart Corcoran

Doctor Dread before he was Doctor Dread. I'm wearing my multicolored pancho I got in Ecuador and am with the first love of my life, Ava Cado.

Here I am leading Bunny Wailer onto stage in Amsterdam. We truly are like brothers and continue to have a respectful rapport in all of our runnings. I feel blessed to have such an intimate relationship with this mystical and deeply rooted individual.

This is my first son, Eric, sitting on the lap of the Cool Ruler, Gregory Isaacs. Like many of the artists I worked with, Gregory felt very close to my family. He even bought little Eric a little toy cell phone.

Buju Banton and I have had some serious reasonings about the Bible and Rastafari as he first made his transformation during his 'Til Shiloh release. He will rise above whatever situation he has found himself in and live for a better day.

Richard Bangham

This 1969 Rolls Royce Silver Shadow was one of the over sixty antique cars I have owned. When Stephen Marley was visiting my house and I asked him if he knew what the *RR* on the hubcaps stood for, he immediately responded, "RAS Records." It further convinced me that this youth has the wisdom of his father running through his veins.

Taylor Branson

Every Christmas I would try to get the family together to take a photo for our annual Christmas card in one of my wacky wagons. This is a very rare 1958 Edsel Bermuda. Notice the "boomerang" tail lights—the most outlandish lights to ever grace an automobile.

I had always wanted to print money, so when I released *Payday* by Culture I figured this would be my chance. We printed up thousands of these stickers and they could be found everywhere, including many musicians' instrument cases.

This is the only record ever put out on the Doctor Dread label. Winston Jarrett decided to release it, and to show his love and respect he chose my name for the record label. "Haile Selassie Is the Chapel," originally sung by Bob Marley and later by his son Stephen.

It was very rare that producer Philip "Fatis" Burrell allowed anyone to take his photograph. But Fatis and I were different. I miss him so very much and have stayed close with his son Kareem.

Bravo

In Kingston at Music Works Studio with Don Carlos and Marcia Griffiths. We were recording a collection of Disney songs for the *Reggae for Kids* series.

Tommy Noonan

At Lion and Fox Studios in Washington, DC with Jim Fox and Eek-A-Mouse. I would typically record my music in Kingston, and then return with the big old twenty-four-track analog tapes to mix them with Jim.

Bill Nowlin

My friend and Rounder Records owner Bill Nowlin talked me into going on a three-week journey through remote Pakistan and China, following the Silk Road upon which Marco Polo had travelled so many centuries earlier. The town of Gil Git in Northern Pakistan would not be safe for Americans to visit in this current time.

Gary Himelfarb

Way back in the day, a friend of mine was serious about growing the best weed possible. He even sent someone to Afghanistan to procure indica seeds when most of the weed you could find was sativa. He farmed on a mountaintop in Virginia right near the West Virginia border, surrounded by tall corn plants. Blessed by the sun and strictly organic. I often wonder why a simple plant that Jah Almighty put on this Earth was ever made illegal.

Sitting on top of the world! I travelled in Peru up to Machu Pichu with Buffy, a close brethren from Jamaica, after we did a show in Lima with Israel Vibration. I would often take side trips to explore places when my artists had engagements in other countries.

My soul mate Roger Steffens called me on his seventy-first birthday while tripping his ass off on LSD. The very same day my *Theremin in Dub* CD arrived at his home, where it became the sound track of his trip. I love Roger dearly.

Making the sign of the heart with a great Jamaican artist, Beres Hammond. Recently I have let Tarrus Riley know I am vexed with him because Beres used to be my favorite Jamaican singer.

Here I am in Kingston with Brigadier Jerry and Charlie Chaplin. When dancehall artists starting endorsing slackness, RAS Records and I and I let ourselves drop behind in the reggae music race. Charlie and Briggy are known as cultural deejays and that was what appealed to me; I and I could not promote deejays who were advocating violence, thuggery, and the mistreatment of women.

Mike Cacia

One of the great personal achievements in my thirty-year music career was producing a CD of Bob Dylan songs done by Jamaican reggae artists. It was my way of introducing Dylan to reggae audiences and reggae to Dylan fans. Toots Hibbert did "Maggie's Farm," which addresses the scandalous nature of slavery, both physical and mental. Bob and Toots met up while on tour, captured in this classic photo taken by my brother Mike Cacia.

This shot was taken backstage at a show which featured Snoop with Stephen Marley and Slightly Stupid. Snoop Dogg had been christened Snoop Lion by Bunny Wailer on a visit to Jamaica; Jah B explained that a dog is a lowly creature but a lion is a king. Snoop and Bunny have had some issues and all is not copasetic within the domain where brethren should dwell together in peace and i-nity.

Jeff Quinton

Eddy Grant was a very cool singer from Barbados best known for his hit song "Electric Avenue." He launched a label, Ice Records, to promote old and new soca recordings, and he asked RAS do his manufacturing and distribution in the US.

I used to know the great Winston Rodney, the Burning Spear, but I do not know him anymore.

Peter Barry

Israel Vibration was the cornerstone of the RAS label. I feel so privileged and honored to have worked so closely with this group and know that my commitment to promoting them and their music had a significant impact on the reggae community worldwide.

Just as I started RAS Records with the purpose of spreading Jamaican culture to the world through music, I have now launched a food company with the intention of spreading Caribbean culture to the world through food. I am hoping to bring the two together and see where this next journey will lead me. Jah guide every time.

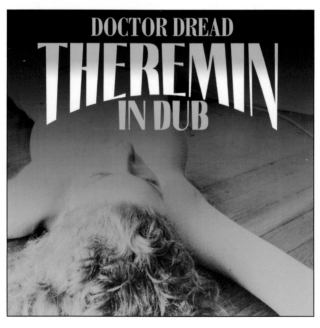

Yes, I did release one CD with Doctor Dread as the featured performer. I became fascinated with the theremin when I discovered it was responsible for the eerie sounds in the Beach Boys' song "Good Vibrations." I learned about the Russian inventor Leon Theremin and ended up buying the finest 1929 RCA theremin from a museum in Florida. I knew it would sound wicked when mixed into some hard-core dub recordings. I recorded this historic CD in 2013 and it has caused some great commotion in both reggae and theremin circles as a new foray into a musical area where no one has gone before.

BUNNY WAILER

In the beginning, there was but one concept,
and that's the concept of I.
Then arose Apollyon, the devil (Satan! Satan!),
claiming that it's you and I.
And from that day on there was trouble in the world,
and the world goin' astray.
—Bunny Wailer, from the song "Amagideon"

Bunny Wailer is one of the deepest and most mystical people I have ever encountered on this Earth. With Jah B, everything is not how it seems. He is connected to the ancient wisdoms that have brought into focus right and wrong, good and bad, yin and yang, and the polarity of the human experience. His never-ending quest to make peace with these diverse emotional realms have caused him to be misunderstood and he has also made some decisions that have not been looked favorably upon by everyone. With someone as complex as Bunny, it is not easy to make blanket statements—often, the black-and-white fades into gray, and reality is something that can only be understood and defended by the man himself.

In the thirty-plus years that Bunny and I have known each other, I've been privileged to have been taken into his confidence and I have learned to accept him for who he is. With his faults and with his goodness and his remarkable ability to perceive things in a way that very few mere mortals are capable of. Yes, he is a living legend. An original Wailer. And his first solo LP, *Blackheart Man*, could be regarded as the best reggae album ever made (including those by Bob Marley) and clearly defines the tenets of Rastafari. If you have never heard it, I suggest you go out and buy a copy today so you can really know what I and I am talking about. Bunny is immortal and his genesis is deep in the unknown places where life itself began.

I first met Bunny in the early 1980s. RAS Records had been distributing some of his records from Sonic Sounds in Jamaica. After releasing three albums with Island Records (including the aforementioned *Blackheart Man*), Bunny had decided to go into business for himself. That is how he has always been: wanting to control every aspect of his business, from the recording to the manufacturing to the distribution. During one of my trips to Jamaica, Neville Lee from Sonic told me to go check Bunny at his father's house, which was just down the road. I remember that day well. Bunny was there drinking a fruit juice concoction he had just made and looked me over and asked how it was that I had come to find him. We talked for a while and I explained to him that RAS was involved in distributing records and that people badly wanted to buy his music in the US, but it was very hard to find.

We made arrangements for me to start buying his records directly from his Solomonic label, and I would always return to the States with loads of Bunny Wailer vinyl. Albums, 12" singles, and 7" singles. I made a point to pay him quickly to help keep his thing going in Jamaica. RAS soon became the largest distributor of the Solomonic label in the United States and Bunny's *Rock 'n' Groove* release was such a big hit that we were buying five hundred copies at a time.

Meanwhile, Jah B had retreated way into the mountains in the parish of Portland to live an ital life, and although he would occasionally come into Kingston he was deeply connected to the natural and spiritual vibes that emanated from that rural environment. He had not performed a show for eight years and the mystery and mystical aura which surrounded him became legendary.

When he announced in 1982 that he would do his first public show in years at the National Stadium in Kingston, I decided this was something I could not miss, and made arrangements to travel to Jamaica. The show was called Youth Consciousness, and it was Bunny's intention to create an uplifting and irie vibe for all who came. To this day it is the best reggae show, including all those Sunsplashes and Reggae on the Rivers, that I have ever witnessed. Youth Consciousness featured Peter Tosh, Gregory Isaacs, Marcia Griffiths, Judy Mowatt, Jimmy Cliff, and of course Bunny Wailer.

I had stopped in Negril on the way there and picked up some of the good Westmoreland draw, and when I saw Peter Tosh backstage I gave him a big bud. He said, "Bwoy, Doctor Dread, anywhere I buck you up in the whole of the world you always bring me the best weed."

And coming from the Bush Doctor, that was a pretty damn good endorsement.

That night I was completely transfixed by Bunny's performance. He had three bands backing him: He started with the Skatalites and did most of his early tracks from the Wailers part of his career. He then shifted into a more rockers-style mode with a band backed by Sly & Robbie. Sly had once shared with me his real secret of making hit music: "Doctor Dread, it is all about the groove. We just make a groove and then the rest just happens." It is one of the most simple yet profound statements anyone ever made to me about music in all my days. And coming from Sly, I knew it was for real.

As daylight began to break, Bunny was launching into "*See the morning sun, ah, ah, ah, on the hillside . . .*" The Roots Radics came on next and Bunny got into the *Rock 'n' Groove* part of the show. The whole thing was spectacular. Eight years without a show and then this tour de force that just blew me away. Bunny was onstage for close to four hours.

He followed this up with a show at Madison Garden in New York City. Bunny always went for broke, and taking on the Garden was something only Bob Marley had ever done in the reggae genre. It sold out! Backstage that night, Bunny might have acknowledged my presence but remained totally unapproachable and intimidating. He cut a daunting figure, usually surrounded by his closest brethren, and even getting an interview was a rare occurrence. After all, he was the Don Dada, Jah B, Bunny Wailer.

Bunny soon signed to Shanachie Records in New Jersey and they began to release most of his product in the States. We still bought a few 7" and 12" singles from Solomonic in Jamaica, but RAS was now principally distributing the Shanachie Bunny Wailer music. Yet Bunny was not happy with how things were going with his publishing over at EMI, and we talked about Tafari Music becoming his publishing administrator. This was over twenty years ago, and Tafari remains his representative on a worldwide basis for his complete catalog. This has been the cornerstone of my relationship with Bunny, and it is remarkable that it has stayed intact all these years. But it was not just handed over to us. We had to prove to Bunny that we were worthy, so he always got all the facts and figures exactly as they had come to me. And as this trust began to grow, it gradually became more than just a business arrangement. We were there to help him in a time of need, and Bunny recognized that it was from the heart and not just from the wallet. At least I hope so.

Sometimes I wonder if Doctor Dread was merely thought of as the goose that laid the golden egg—and of course you would not want to kill off or harm an animal of that nature. Because of my relaxed and worry-free manner, many people in Jamaica felt I had lots of money. They mostly all respected me, but I never left Jamaica with a dime in my pocket. Bunny would call and say he was looking for a carrot. Or he was as broke as a church mouse. And although many times it sounded desperate, it never felt threatening. And if I was straight with him and told him I could not help him, he was cool about it and still gave thanks. If we made a big score with one of his songs, we would let him know about it right away and usually advance him the money before we even received it ourselves. Lots of money flowed through my hands into Bunny's, as his publishing was a constant stream of revenue.

The spring which fed the stream was of course his remarkable repertoire of songs, especially "Electric Boogie," which he wrote for Marcia Griffiths and was used in so many commercials and movies that it became one of our top-grossing releases. Bunny and I began to spend a lot more time together in Jamaica and would have long reasonings about life that may have started with cursing and bloodclatting about something but usually ended with hearty laughing and good vibes.

At one point he had separated from his tour manager Bo Edwards and he came to my hotel in Kingston and told me of the circumstances, so we talked about me working with him in a managerial capacity. He also told me of the enormous burden he felt in being the only surviving Wailer, and that many people had wanted Bob and Peter dead, and it might be the same for him. I did not realize it then, but he felt responsible for protecting the Wailers' name.

Years later he would reveal to me the fullness of what this meant. He would tell me of how he and Bob, at five and six years old, would ride on donkeys in the hills of St. Ann at Nine Miles and round up the cows each evening. How he and Bob grew up as brothers, and how his dad had had a child with Bob's mother. About their time in Trenchtown together, and how Peter Tosh was recruited to form the mighty trio that became known as the Wailers. And how these very same Wailers had gone through the learning process under Coxsone Dodd at Studio One and later with Lee "Scratch" Perry to eventually form their own record label, Tuff Gong. The Power of this Trinity was strong and Bunny always referred to Bob and Peter as his brothers.

Then Chris Blackwell entered the picture and Bob, Peter, and Bunny were signed to Island Records. But after some touring in America and England, Bunny dropped out. The pay and the conditions did not suit his temperament, and his mistrust of Chris Blackwell also factored into this decision. The first Wailers album on Island, *Catch a Fire*, had been met with great fanfare worldwide, followed by *Burnin'*. But after Bunny left the group, Chris began to change things up. He began to call the *backing* band the Wailers, and reissued both of these albums as "Bob Marley and the Wailers." How could this be? Bob, Peter, and Bunny had been the Wailers. How could someone just come and steal your name? All subsequent albums and all mention of Bob Marley was always referred to as Bob Marley and the Wailers. Even today there are multiple groups that tour as the Wailers, and some just have one member of the original band that backed Bob, Peter, and Bunny.

Bunny took this slight personally, and he brought the pain inside of himself, which explains in part his reclusiveness and mistrust of others. He had been turned off by the vulgarities of the music business, with its ruthless profit-driven impulse, and instead found sanctuary in his personal life, through a closer connection to Rastafari and a pure and holistic lifestyle. After the passing of Bob and then Peter, it was just Bunny left to defend the truth. Bunny trusted me and knew I was capable when it came to business and negotiating on his behalf. If there's one thing I can credit for my long success in

the music business, it's the fact that I'm able to understand the sentiments, eccentricities, and the creative
side of the artists while still being able to handle art as
a business; it's a fine line to walk.

Bunny ended up sharing all sorts of anecdotes from
his rich life. Of how, when he had completed *Blackheart
Man*, Chris Blackwell could not live without the LP. How
their negotiations became very heated, as Bunny held
firm while Chris wanted it for the least he could pay.
Chris had his lawyer come in from England and Bunny
gave him some weed to smoke and the lawyer got so
blitzed he ended up on the floor unable to communicate. (Jah B could come up with some good weed; when
High Times magazine visited Jamaica to do a feature on
Jamaican herb they ended up concluding that Bunny
Wailer had the best product in all of the country.) The
lawyer was flat out, and when Bunny finally agreed to
sign the contract he made the lawyer add the clause that
once Chris Blackwell dies, all rights would revert back
to Bunny Wailer. When relating all of this to me, Bunny
chuckled and said, "Now I can get back the rights anytime I want." He even told me that Chris had once transformed himself into a bat to beat him in a race up some
stairs at a hotel in Ocho Rios; their adversarial relationship remains in full force to this day. The last time I saw
Chris Blackwell was at a book signing in Washington,
DC. Despite his outward charm, charisma, and powers
of persuasion, his wax exterior is beginning to melt away,
revealing the soulless apparition that fills his being.

Of course, my time touring with Bunny had its ups
and downs. It is true that Jah B really loved to be in Jamaica, and if not for the good money his rare overseas

performances earned for him, he would probably prefer to just chill inna yard. He had a reputation for not showing up for shows, as for Bunny it was all about vibes. Or signs that told him this or that. If a bird fell off a wire dead the day before he was to leave Jamaica for a show, this was enough of a sign for him to not get on the plane. Some people said he was afraid of the iron bird, but on the many occasions I have flown with him I've never detected this type of phobia. He knew he was in Jah's hands and endured his time from takeoff to landing without too much consternation.

At first I set up some mini-tours of just three dates because I did not want to lay too much on Bunny in one go-around. His performance fee was very high, and he required the promoters to pay for airfares, hotels, and even securing visas. I also knew I had to be out there with him, since the slightest wrong move on anyone's part could turn Bunny off to the whole thing and he would just shut down. "The World According to Bunny Wailer." If it made sense to him, then why shouldn't it make sense to everyone else?

All business details were reviewed with Jah B before he felt free to just perform. His reputation for doing shows of over three hours was sometimes a problem, as certain promoters had curfews and getting him off the stage could be a nightmare. Remember, it's all about the vibes. And if Bunny is feeling the vibes he can go on and on and on. He is the Energizer Bunny. And on tour he would smoke his weed out of a big carrot. Cut off the bottom and carve out a pipe and use the tube from a pen as the stem. Whenever I told the promoter to have a big fat carrot for us when we landed, they didn't know whether to take me seriously, but I told them to just make sure. Getting him off the stage was the problem, and there were numerous occasions when I was standing on the side of the stage with an increasingly anxious promoter trying to signal him or the trumpet player Barry to let Bunny know his time was up. Sometimes it worked and sometimes it didn't.

One time at a big festival in Long Beach, California, Bunny ran past curfew. The bass player had fallen asleep at the hotel and did not make it to the gig on time and we were very late getting onstage. Bunny was determined to play his full set and refused to cut it short. It cost us a few thousand dollars in fines and put a strain on my relationship with the promoter. But not even the great Doctor Dread tells Bunny what to do.

The same thing had happened at Reggae on the River with my good friends Carol Bruno and Carl T and myself trying to flag down Bunny to come off stage. He had walked the grounds of Reggae on the River with me earlier that day and declared, "This is how reggae should be presented." There were people camping along a big river with redwoods all around and reggae going for three nights. It was also in the heart of Humboldt County where the best sinse in America was being grown. Carol Bruno and her partner PB did an amazing job staging this festival for over twenty years and it became an annual pilgrimage for me. Bunny was in the vibe that night and he was the closing act. It was like he was performing Holy Communion onstage and the audience was all receiving the sacraments he was handing out. I witnessed this from the audience and was transfixed by the sheer power Bunny was capable of bringing forth. But getting him off that stage proved impossible, and eventually Carol had to pull the plug and call it a night.

We had numerous other one- or two-week tours, and both the band and Bunny were pleased with how things were going. Doctor Dread was now regarded as a person who promoters could count on to make sure that Bunny would show up for his gigs, and the offers rolled in. I would negotiate the fees based on parameters that Bunny and I had established. And Bunny was very generous with me, always paying me what I had asked for. I took care of all aspects of the tour including getting visas, booking and paying for airfares, arranging transportation, paying the musicians their salaries and per diems, dealing with the promoters regarding hospitality and settlement, and just making sure everyone was feeling good about being on the road. At one point I earned the ultimate compliment from the band when they told me that they did not consider me a white man. I used to joke with some RAS artists and ask them why they treated me like a white man, and they would always laugh.

We did a three-week run with Ziggy and Stephen Marley consisting of seventeen shows in twenty-one days. I believe it was the most strenuous tour of Jah B's entire career. The vibes were GREAT. Ziggy and Steve referred to Jah B as "Uncle Bunny," and they all joined up on stage at the conclusion of each show to perform "Get Up, Stand Up" together. Bunny's band, the Solomonic Reggaestra, were enthusiastic about this long run with its first-class everything, and we really were one big happy family traveling from one side of the country to the other.

The tour culminated in Washington, DC, and I

booked everyone's flights so they could have an extra day off to celebrate at my house in Maryland. Jah B is a master chef, and he was going to cook up an ital feast. Ziggy and his band moved on to another gig but Steve and Bunny and their band members enjoyed a party none of us can ever forget. Jah B always cooked for everyone on tour, and often the musicians would parade to his room to get a good taste of his cornmeal porridge or other soups and fish.

Bunny cooked his ass off that day. Fish tea. Turned cornmeal with fish. Escoveitch fish. The kitchen was blazing and everyone celebrated a tour that had gone smooth and without problems. I had invited some close friends and the Rastafari Elders of Washington also blessed us with their presence. Steve Marley's tour bus was parked in front of my house, and while many Rastas sat around my yard and reasoned and clouds of marijuana smoke drifted through the air, I wondered what my neighbors might be thinking. But I was too busy cooking up jerk chicken and jerk red snapper. I had been bragging to the band about how my jerk chicken was as good as anything they could get in Jamaica, so I was working the grill hard that day too.

Word got out about how well that tour went and how Bunny was able to sustain three weeks on the road. He was contacted by Michel from Media Sept in France, who was one of the principal people responsible for bringing reggae artists to Europe. He was organizing a tour with Capleton and Third World and wanted to add Bunny Wailer to the bill. Like many other promoters before him, he went to Jamaica and made direct contact with Bunny. This had become standard procedure: people would negotiate directly with Bunny, and when things broke down they would call me. In a way it was amusing because I rarely found Bunny to be a difficult person to deal with. Like the time *GQ* magazine called frantically at the last minute wanting to set up a photo shoot; they were freaking out, and couldn't understand why Bunny wasn't cooperating or letting them take his picture. I was offended and irritated: why would they call me *after* the shit hit the fan? So I can clean it all up? They had known about this article for months but didn't bother to reach out earlier. So I said to them, "Sorry, I'm not going to help you—you need to figure this one out on your own."

Needless to say, Bunny never took the photo. But this kind of thing happened all the time. Though I never liked to call myself his manager, this is the de facto position I developed over the years. I knew Bunny well enough to be able to present situations to him so he would be comfortable with what he was putting himself into. And the fact is, in our celebrity-obsessed, money-driven culture, Bunny is often the least unreasonable person in the room—as in the case of *GQ*.

Anyway, Michel from Europe became so frustrated that even though he did not initially want to include me in the scenario, he eventually realized that I was the one who could help get Bunny on his tour. We soon got everything sorted out and I let Bunny know all was cool.

But first we had to complete a short tour of California and Hawaii with Steel Pulse. Moss Jacobs was the promoter and he could not figure out a way to fill Bunny's time for four days between the California part and Hawaii, and was considering just having Bunny do the California leg. I suggested that we could just cover our own expenses for the four nights off in San Francisco. Bunny never cared about fancy hotels as his ghetto vibe and upbringing made him understand that a clean bed and clean bathroom were all that was necessary to get you through the night. Bob Marley had sung, *"Cold ground was my bed last night and rock was my pillow too . . ."* So fancy hotels were not required when we traveled, and I sometimes used this as leverage to get the promoters to pay us more money for the shows.

Those four days off in San Francisco were very enjoyable. Bunny rarely left his hotel room. He would cook and smoke weed and get visits from close brethren sometimes, but generally he kept to himself. He told me in all his years of touring he never brought a woman back to his hotel room. Jah B was in his own space, even if surrounded by others. A friend of a friend had brought down a huge bag of some serious weed from the mountains of Northern California and I remember Carl T walking out of the bathroom of Bunny's room and hitting the floor. This was some powerful smoke, and even Bunny commented on its super strength. I took a bunch of the band members on the streetcars down to Fisherman's Wharf and bought them all some delicious soup. It made me feel good to see them enjoying the world outside of Jamaica, and since I was not someone who liked being holed up in my hotel room I would often venture out with band members and try and give them an idea of what a foreign country was like. To broaden their horizons while I was doing the same thing for myself.

When we got to Hawaii I received an itinerary for the European tour. I had been asking for a while and it finally got to us. I noticed there was a two-day trip to Israel, and Michel was also suggesting we do a date in Réunion Island off the coast of East Africa at the end of the tour. We were getting paid by the week and it seemed a little over the top to ask us to break out of Europe for these other shows. I explained to Bunny that Michel was trying to get us to go to Israel right in the middle of the tour. Bunny asked if Israel was part of Europe, and when I told him it was not, he was adamant about not going there. Bunny said that we would not be treated like "human cargo"; that he had negotiated with Michel for a tour of Europe, and that it was to Europe and Europe alone he would tour. I related this information to Michel and he was not pleased. He said all the other artists on the tour had agreed to go to Israel.

But Bunny was not the *other* artists. If Michel had insisted that Bunny make this trip, then Bunny would have just canceled the tour. Bunny also refused to travel to Italy since he still harbored resentment over Mussolini's invasion of Ethiopia during World War II, and he wouldn't fly through London because of England's participation in the Iraq War. Even I thought he was being unreasonable, but we were dealing with the World According to Bunny.

We booked Bunny and his brethren Patrick to fly through Miami and then on to Paris. The rest of the band had come through London and arrived in Paris the day before the first show. Bunny somehow missed his flight and the promoter and I went into panic mode waiting for their arrival at Charles de Gaulle Airport in

Paris. I had received no communication from Bunny and although I kept assuring the promoter he would come, deep down inside I grew increasingly nervous. They ended up being routed through London (the same place Bunny said he wouldn't fly through) to Paris to begin the tour, and I greeted them at the airport. Bunny's close childhood friend and photographer Patrick Blackwood smiled upon seeing me, and said to Bunny, "I told you Doc would be here waiting for us." And as we sped down the motorway making sure we could get Bunny to the venue on time to perform his first show of the tour, it was pure excitement and discussion about the travel ordeal they had just endured. Again, I gave thanks to Jah that Bunny had arrived safely and that the tour could now commence.

Jah B was performing well and we were all having a great tour. Often Patrick and I would roam the towns as I wanted to make the most of my time in Europe and liked to get to know the places I was visiting. In Marseille, after tucking in the band at our hotel for the night, I ventured down to the port and found a nice café where I ordered a bowl of bouillabaisse that changed my life.

This was two major tours in a row for Bunny, and it was frankly one of the most enjoyable trips I had ever been on. Jah B and I got very close during our late-night tour bus reasonings—I even took the rap for the band when our bus was pulled over in France and searched by drug-sniffing dogs, which somehow managed to find our well-hidden stash. It was like receiving a traffic ticket with a small fine, but they did keep the weed and warned me if I was busted again in France the charges would be more severe. In any case, even though I had recently been let go from my job at Sanctuary, I was making good money on the road with Bunny and digging the European lifestyle.

After these two tours we did several more small shows and a few one-off performances. Bunny was showing up and performing well and all was good. But he was still setting things up on his own. He had arranged a tour of Australia through Dave Betteridge in London, who was coordinating directly with the promoter in Australia. Betteridge had been an important booking agent for reggae acts back in the day, and may even have set up some Bob Marley dates at one time. But he had once booked a tour with Israel Vibration after they signed to RAS and was fucking around with our money. That is one thing I will not tolerate. Don't fuck around with my money. If you owe me fifty bucks, just pay me. Don't give me some lame-ass excuse as to why this or why that. Just pay me the fucking money. I came down hard over the phone to Dave in England and he actually started crying! So when Bunny told me he was working with Dave Betteridge and was running into problems, I was not surprised.

Again I was called in to try and straighten out the situation, and I talked directly with the promoter in Australia and attempted to structure a compensation element for Betteridge. But things could not get worked out and Bunny ended up cancelling the entire tour. I returned the advance Bunny had received for the tour with money he was owed by my publishing company, and that was that.

But then things went from bad to worse. We had been contacted by Byron Malcolm in Miami to do a string of dates in Brazil. Bunny had never been there, though I knew the Brazilian people would adore him and we could develop this market for him. I had been there on a few occasions with Israel Vibration and loved the country and its people and its culture. And Brazil loved reggae.

Byron had arranged with the top promoter in Brazil to do five shows. He was the same promoter who had brought the Rolling Stones there. I knew we were in good hands, as Byron had worked with Inner Circle for many years and the promoter in Brazil was top notch. We agreed to a fee and the contract stipulated that we would be paid 100 percent of it before anyone left Jamaica. This way there was no risk to us. But we never received the final payment in time and the tour was canceled. We made arrangements with the promoter to reschedule the tour with an additional charge for them not sticking to the terms of the original contract.

New terms and conditions were worked out and the tour was finally rescheduled. But two days before we were set to leave, Bunny announced he would not be going. There was another reggae tour going around Brazil at the same time as ours. It was a group that bassist Fully Fullwood had put together of Peter Tosh's band members. And Junior Marvin, former lead guitarist of Bob Marley's backing band, was touring as "the Wailers." Our promoter did not want to compete with this tour so he was putting all the acts together and came up with a Wailers "tribute package" promoting the names Bob Marley, Bunny Wailer, and Peter Tosh. Bunny was furious. He said neither Junior Marvin nor Fully Fullwood had the right to use the Marley or Tosh name, and that only the offspring of these former Wailers (his brothers) had the right to tour and make money off their names.

"Please, Bunny, I am begging you. I can assure you that once we are there we can straighten everything out and make things right. Too much work has gone into this and I know the promoter will have everything just right for us."

I had never begged nobody for nothing, but this time I was begging. I could not face another canceled tour with Jah B. It almost felt like *my* credibility was on the line. But Bunny was adamant; he was not going.

One week later I got a job back in the seafood business and gave up the idea of booking shows for Bunny. I immediately returned the $7,500 I had kept for myself, though the balance of the $75,000 that had been advanced to Bunny had already been spent.

Bunny could go through money quicker than anyone I've ever known. But it was his money and it was none of my business how he wanted to spend it. I once told him that he must have read in the Bible that it is easier for a camel to pass through the eye of a needle than for a rich man to enter the gates of Zion, and that this must have made a strong impression on him. After all, he had no bank account. He said, "Why would anyone ever keep money in a bank? Money is for spending. To make use of." I could not argue, but it factored into the reason he was always broke.

Many of his big expenditures came from a place of wanting to help others, though they often turned out to be poor business decisions. He reopened Skateland in New Kingston so the youth of Jamaica could have good wholesome fun during a time when violence had become commonplace. He spent lots of money fixing up the place and was proud of it, but the community never supported it and it fell back into disrepair. He then opened a Rastafari school in an uptown area of Kingston and offered courses in African history, and would even come there each day and cook healthy food for the youth. He leased the land from descendants of the Marcus Garvey family, and paid for repairs after a hurricane caused severe damage to the property. But the landlord did not agree with the repairs and they quarreled over this and the school was closed. He also had a dream (some Jamaicans refer to this as a vision) that there was buried treasure on his land in Portland. Way up in the hills. There was an opening to a cave and he had visioned great amounts of buried treasure that pirates had hidden there. I arranged for a group of spelunkers to come in from California and Bunny treated them like gold, and they went down into this cave but there was nothing there. Jah B simply had to satisfy his curiosity.

RAS Records also became involved with Bunny's record label when his agreements with Shanachie began to expire. My first release was from a group known as Psalms. These were Jah B's backup singers and they always toured with us. I paid him a $15,000 advance for this CD even though I figured I would never make it back. It was my way of beginning work with Bunny to represent his Solomonic catalog and to show him that RAS could be a good partner. The CD never sold well but then Bunny approached me about releasing a fifty-track, two-CD set of Bob Marley songs to celebrate what would have been the fiftieth birthday of his late brother. Jah B had already done a few Bob Marley tribute CDs, and I wanted to support his celebration of Bob's music, so I agreed to pay him the whopping sum of $75,000 as an advance. I sensed that my relationship with Bunny would always bring in money, though I also knew that going into the studio to work on such a massive project would be a costly endeavor.

I will admit that in some ways I am not a very astute businessman, and that I just do things based on vibes, and somehow Jah has always looked out over me. The musicians knew Doctor Dread had financed this recording, but Bunny remained in complete control of all aspects of his releases, from the production down to the record jacket.

My promotion department put out the word and we began publicizing the release. This double CD went on to earn a Grammy Award for Bunny and RAS, and I feel honored to have had the opportunity to begin work with Jah B on this kind of level. Although we had a number of recordings nominated for a Grammy, this was the only time we ever won. I knew that the love Bunny had for Bob went into this, and I could hear it in his vocals. On the business side, I learned even more about the importance of investing in artists and their careers: the more you invest in an artist, the more potential you'll have to get a larger return—this is something I would keep in mind when signing new artists.

But Bunny's obsessive need for money was always overwhelming him, and he could be relentless in his requests for more and more and more. Sometimes I would send him thousands of dollars, and by the next week he would be calling again. He had an uncanny sense of knowing when we had received money on his behalf. And his anger at the injustices that had been levied upon the Wailers, along with those he witnessed in everyday life in Jamaican society, created a struggle inside of his being which pitted good against evil, right against wrong. Just like in the lyrics to his song "Amagideon." He knew of Satan and he knew of the Heavenly Father. We would have long talks about both of these forces, and these often-heated conversations would usually end in some laughing, and Jah B's humility and love would resurface.

Later I did a small tour in California with Bunny, and he asked me to negotiate a few shows for him in Argentina and Spain. Both guarantees were significant and the promoters sent the money in advance. But Bunny canceled again and said an illness prevented him from appearing, though he would only tell me it had to do with some tooth pain. At this point I was more absorbed in my job in the seafood business (more on this later) and knew that I had to take care of my family, and that because of the frequency of canceled shows with Bunny I could no longer get involved with his bookings. He did ask me to negotiate his fee for Jazz Fest in New Orleans last year, and I just turned it over to the booking agent Paul LaMonica; if he wanted to work things out with Bunny, he could, but without my involvement. And all the other calls and e-mails I would get asking about Bunny performing, I'd just refer directly to him.

I heard of other canceled shows but I was becoming far removed and could not understand why people would continue to book Bunny and advance him money when he had not left Jamaica for over two years. I was concerned about his health issues, though he never went into depth about them with me. Do I think it was wrong to take money to do shows and then not return it? Yes, I do. But I also think Bunny could not help himself. I think he believed when he negotiated and took the money that his intentions were to go through with it and perform the show, but something would get in the way and he'd back out. It was that struggle going on inside of him. It is so complex and difficult to explain, but perhaps the lyrics from his songs express it best.

I have always accepted Jah B for who he is. And with that comes the right and the wrong. Only Jah is perfect, and Jah B, as with the rest of us, falls short of this perfection of His Holiness. Bunny Wailer has been both blessed and cursed by the Creator. But if he calls on me as a friend, I will of course be there for him as much as I can be. I don't desert my friends, especially in times of need.

Bunny's recent situation with Snoop Dogg (who Bunny renamed "Snoop Lion") has again put him in a position where he is misunderstood and people are not able to see the full picture. He told Snoop that a dog is a lowly creature and that a lion is a king, and that if Snoop were to make a serious commitment to the Rastafari way of life, Bunny would christen him Snoop Lion. But just because you smoke a lot of weed and you dig reggae and you wear red, gold, and green does not make you a Rasta. And Snoop's allegation that he is Bob Marley reincarnated seem a little far-fetched to me. Still, whatever business arrangements Jah B and Snoop discussed were between them. Some people think Bunny is trying to throw a wrench into Snoop's conversion to Rastafari. Bunny has his side of the story and I guess you can believe whatever you want.

When he explained his half of the story, I made the mistake of saying to Bunny, "I know how you feel." He replied tersely, "So you think you are Bunny Wailer?" I shouldn't have been surprised by his reaction, since this is after all the man who wrote the song "Who Feels It Knows It" (later popularized by both Bob and Rita Marley)—how can anyone know how someone else actually feels, especially someone as complicated and with as interesting a life as Bunny Wailer?

It has been both an amazing privilege and an exercise in perseverance in having my life so intertwined with Bunny Wailer, and I give thanks for all the good and interesting times we have endured. I can only wish Jah B the very best and pray for his salvation. Jah guide and protect. Every time.

OH DOCTOR, PLEASE HELP ME

Oh help me, please doctor, I'm damaged . . .
—Mick Jagger, from "Dear Doctor"

My second son Ian was born on June 19, 1995, and my oldest son Eric turned five on July 24 of that year. That year the heat and humidity between Washington, DC, and Baltimore was out of control. One day during that oppressive summer I was taking Eric to an Orioles game with my father-in-law who lived walking distance from Camden Yards. Eric was a big Cal Ripken fan and going to see a ballgame with him was always a great time for me. Baseball was important in our household: I always made time to play catch with my kids each morning, and coached and attended my sons' Little League games.

So I was getting ready to make the drive to Baltimore with Eric and had complained to my wife that my teeth were really hurting, and she advised me to see a dentist the first chance I got. Eric and I drove to Baltimore and my teeth continued to hurt, and when I explained to my father-in-law that I did not feel well and that maybe just he and Eric should go to the game, he expressed concern. He had been a pulmonologist most of his life in Binghamton, New York, and was now the medical director of Maryland General Hospital in Baltimore. He said we should go to the emergency room there just to be safe, and I was feeling so unwell that I agreed.

It appeared from my EKG that there might be a slight problem with my heart, but I was assured that it was probably nothing serious. They wanted to keep me overnight and have a cardiologist take a closer look at the test. I was put into their cardiac care unit and then the next morning taken by ambulance to another hospital nearby. I still felt lousy but I was not sure why all this fuss was being made over what I was repeatedly told was probably nothing.

When I got to MedStar Union Memorial Hospital the doctor there wanted to conduct an angiogram. This is where they put a catheter into a vein in your thigh and push it up into your heart so they can examine the condition of your arteries and look for blockages. I was awake for the whole procedure. The cardiologist informed me that I had three severe blockages in my heart, and the tooth pain I had been feeling was actually jaw pain, which was a classic symptom of someone getting ready to have a heart attack. There was no damage to the heart muscle, but it seemed as though a heart attack was imminent. He advised that I should have heart bypass surgery immediately or I could be dead within a matter of hours. Tears began to run down the side of my face. "I am only forty years old. How is this possible?" It was a kind of protest, but I also knew it was futile. He explained the seriousness of the situation and I agreed to the surgery and told them to wake me up when it was over. I could not believe this was happening to me.

I now realized why they had brought me over to Union Memorial Hospital: they did open-heart surgery there, and since Doctor Manzari was my father-in-law I was getting some very special treatment. Within an hour of my angiogram I was rushed into the operating room. Doctor Mispareta had earned the reputation of being an excellent open-heart surgeon in DC and Baltimore. He had also performed surgery on my dad, so history was unfortunately repeating itself in a way.

It is my understanding that they remove your heart from your body and keep it beating and still connected while they replace the clogged arteries. For my surgery they took arteries from my chest instead of my legs as these are usually stronger and last longer. These days they use stents much more often than bypass surgery since they don't have to crack you open to get to your heart. They just slip in the stents to open up your arteries while they are doing the angiogram. It seems almost routine now to get a few stents and then be on your way and back to work.

Open-heart surgery is a different beast. I remember waking in a fog with tubes down my throat and three tubes in the area above my stomach. The doctors came in and pulled the ribbed tube from my throat, which was a strange sensation I will never forget. I remember my father-in-law coming in and me thanking him for saving my life and telling him I loved him. This was my first memory after the surgery.

I also remember seeing my dad in the same situation. It had scared the shit out of me—he had looked like death. And even though I was a healthy eater (no pork or meat for over thirty-five years) and kept to a natural diet, I had inherited my father's genes and heart disease was included in the package. If you think that the one having the surgery is going through the worst, you are wrong; the worry and concern of the family is greater. So I can only imagine the fear my family must have felt, especially my wife Deb, with a newborn child to take care of and a five-year-old who had just come down with chicken pox. All at the same time. God bless her and her fortitude to endure all this emotional turmoil that had been heaped upon her.

Slowly I recovered. From intensive care I was put into a private room. I was still very weak. I began to eat and eventually was allowed to leave my bed to go to the bathroom. I recall waking one morning in the hospital with an erection and starting to believe that I might eventually be okay again. It gave me hope and I laughed. But another day I went to the bathroom and all the emergency alarms on my monitor started to go off. My heartbeat had raced up to over 180 beats per minute and I was in severe danger. I was rushed back into intensive care and they managed to get my heart rate under control. In Jamaica a well-known saying is, *One step forward, two steps backward*, and that was how I was feeling. My heart began behaving erratically with my BPM all over the place: sometimes slow, sometimes fast. And my heart was also going into arrhythmia off and on.

After about ten days, still very weak from my ordeal, I was finally released from the hospital and went home in the care of Debbie. With a lengthy recovery process ahead of me, that night I had a dream I was swimming in the ocean, just beyond the waves. Beams of sunlight from between the clouds were drawing me up into heaven. I woke with a start after being shaken by Debbie, who had grown concerned by the noises I was making. Perhaps if Debbie hadn't woken me up that night I might have made the transition to the other side . . . Thankfully that didn't happen, and a few nights later I had a dream I was having sex with Uma Thurman (don't even ask). But she started crying, then told me she had AIDS. Another example of the fear of death manifesting itself in my subconscious.

All of this happened when I was working with Rounder Records, who had pretty much given me complete freedom to run the label and distribution company as I saw fit. As long as RAS was making money, Rounder just allowed things to roll along and pretty much left me alone. The three owners were extremely understanding and sympathetic to my medical condition and encouraged me to take the time I needed to recover. I had some people at work who were capable of running the distribution company and the label took a brief hiatus as I healed. My house was less than a mile from our warehouse and offices so it was not too hard for me to make the occasional visit to rally the troops and let everyone know I was on the road to recovery. And thanks to visits from good friends like Fatis and Luciano, who would check up on me and spread positive vibes, I was able to keep my spirits up.

Before long, I was back at work going full-time and continuing to build up RAS. I was amazed at how well I had recovered. I was playing rigorous tennis on a regular basis and working out and felt very fit. I had to thank Jah for making all of this possible.

Then, without warning, seventeen years later during a tour with Bunny and the Marley brothers, my heart acted up again. I had taken two days off from the tour to be with my family back in Washington while the bus carried the rest of the band north to Boston. Even though much time had passed, I immediately knew what it was: atrial fib. It really had me freaked out. After seven or eight hours my irregular heartbeat subsided and I told Deb about it and I think we both just felt it was brought on by the strenuous tour, facing the grueling demands of being on the road—we had seventeen shows scheduled in twenty-one days.

I felt better the next day, but one month later the arrhythmia came back with a vengeance. It rocked my world. Another eight-hour episode and it wiped me out so bad I had to spend the entire next day in bed just to recover. I needed a cardiologist and I needed one quick.

My good friend Marc Appelbaum and his wife Liz always raved about their general practitioner/cardiologist, so I called Doctor Dwyer the next day. At his first open appointment a couple of months later, he confirmed that I was once again suffering from arrhythmia, an irregular heartbeat. He said it had nothing to do with the tour I had been on. It had just decided to rear its ugly head so many years after my surgery, and was caused by a nerve sending out an electrical impulse that fired at an irregular interval and made the heart jump. The only real danger (besides the discomfort it caused) was that it could lead to clotting and I could have a stroke (and die). Nothing major.

He immediately put me on a blood thinner and started me on a regimen of medicine to try to keep the irregular heartbeat in check. Unfortunately, the medicine really fucked with me. I was tired all the time. I had no energy. No sex drive. No nothing. It seemed that I needed to lick the fib problem before I could think about returning to my routine.

So I was out of work, physically compromised with arrhythmia, and trying to figure out where to go from there. Every time the fib hit me, it hit me hard. The meds were not working. Doctor Dwyer told me about a procedure called an ablation. He explained that the doctors would use a catheter to reach into my heart and fry the parts that were sending out the signals that threw my heart into arrhythmia. He said I should go and see Doctor Andrea Natale at the world-famous Cleveland Clinic, as he was the top surgeon on the planet performing this procedure.

I flew out to Cleveland for my initial appointment, and when I landed there I saw huge posters all over the walls extolling the virtues of the clinic. Eight-foot pictures of their great doctors and the miracles they performed. And there was one of Doctor Andrea Natale, heralded as the greatest of all ablationists in the world. I felt lucky to be able to meet with him.

The doctor explained he could do the procedure but that he was completely booked up and the earliest he could schedule me was about a year from then. For me this was unacceptable. I told him I was leaving in two days on a three-week European tour (again with Bunny Wailer), but that getting this taken care of was paramount—I could not afford to wait another year. I have always had a hard time taking no for an answer, so I continued to push for him to find time for me. He had his nurse recheck his schedule and saw he had an opening in late September and could fit me in then. So I went and did a great tour all across Europe with Bunny headlining a show that also featured Capleton and Third World.

September arrived and Deb and I flew out to Cleveland. Getting ready to go into the OR, I saw another gentleman sitting there in his wheelchair wearing a hospital gown. I asked what he was in for and he said he had a six thirty a.m. appointment with Doctor Natale to receive an ablation. I found this to be unusual and did not understand how the two of us could be scheduled for ablations with Doctor Natale at the same time, but I didn't dwell on it.

I was put on an operating table and a doctor came in and explained that the procedure would take about three hours and I would be under for the whole time— but still no sign of Doctor Natale. There was nothing I could say. I was laid out on the table with a bunch of tubes hooked up to me and had signed a consent form, so there was no backing out now.

When I finally came out of it I was wheeled to the recovery room and reunited with Deb. Doctor Natale eventually showed up and said he thought things went pretty well but was not 100 percent sure. By the time we got back home to Washington, DC, I was very weak and still had trouble breathing. I called Doctor Dwyer to explain the symptoms I was experiencing, and he sent me to Sibley Hospital the very next day for some additional tests.

After extensive X-rays, the doctor at Sibley explained that in some rare cases the phrenic nerve is hit during an ablation and this can freeze up the diaphragm, causing only one side of a lung to function. He said this could typically take up to one year to heal on its own. This was not good news. I called the Cleveland Clinic a few days later and was told that Doctor Natale "no longer works here," that his contract had not been renewed. What the fuck? My whole state of being began spinning. When I asked what had happened to Doctor Natale, the woman explained that she was not at liberty to discuss this. Feeling very confused, I searched the Internet for any information I could find regarding his sudden departure from the Cleveland Clinic.

Turns out this was major news in the Cleveland *Plain Dealer*. Evidently he had been let go due to conflicts related to his outside work with other medical facilities. I had told Deb that the whole day of the surgery did not feel right, and to this day, though I have no proof, I do not believe it was him who actually performed it.

Meanwhile, my cardiologist in DC grew increasingly concerned. He was pissed about my frozen diaphragm and the fact that Doctor Natale, who he had recommended, was no longer at the Cleveland Clinic. I was still having trouble breathing. We all take breathing for granted, but imagine if you cannot breathe: Walking up the stairs would completely take my breath away. Anytime I went to lay down or eat I would start coughing uncontrollably. I struggled to breathe. Do you even fucking know what I am talking about?

I was told I would need to return to the Cleveland Clinic for additional tests. Afterward, a doctor there explained that these tests showed how two of my pulmonary arteries had also been collapsed during the ablation, and I was only getting 30 percent of the oxygen my lungs required. No wonder I couldn't breathe. Things were going from bad to worse.

I was told I would need to go back to the Cleveland Clinic (again) for a rare procedure from a *pediatric* cardiologist. Nearly all the cases of collapsed pulmonary arteries occurred in babies born with a defect—along with less than 1 percent of patients who receive ablations (lucky me!). The thought of returning to the Cleveland Clinic was throwing me into another place. It was like I had entered *The Twilight Zone*. Deb and I sat there holding hands, not knowing what to think.

Then Minerva, a nurse I had gotten close to during this process, shared another bombshell: the ablation procedure had also lodged a large blood clot into my heart, and this could kill me at any moment. Deb and I just sat there and cried; I needed to get this dealt with right away. What the fuck was going on? What had really happened that fateful day in September? While these questions swirled around in my head I went into orbit, and thank God Deb was there to provide the gravitational pull to keep me tethered to the Earth.

For the next month, I had to inject a heavy-duty blood thinner into my stomach twice a day to try to break up the clot. At any moment it could dislodge itself and result in a stroke or worse—death. Imagine walking around with a large blood clot in your heart and not knowing where the sucker might end up.

By this time I was so sick of hospitals. So sick of the smell. So sick of being hooked up to drips to infuse me with dyes and nuclear isotopes. So sick of being told everything is going to be okay and then it not turning out that way. And like Frankenstein's monster, I had been electroshocked back into a normal heartbeat countless times.

After another month I was now cleared to have my surgery back at the Cleveland Clinic. I will admit that I was extremely apprehensive (i.e., scared as shit) about returning and having this rare surgical procedure, but I felt confident about the new doctor and she had some excellent credentials. I told Bunny Wailer about the procedure and explained everything that had happened to me, and he assured me that the hands of Jah would be guiding the hands of the doctors as they performed the surgery. I'll never forget Bunny's words, which he meant from the heart; they gave me more comfort and assurance than I had received from anyone else.

After the operation I awoke in an intensive care unit in the pediatric ward, surrounded by toys and Disney wallpaper. They kept me around a few days to make sure I would be able to breathe on my own without oxygen, and then discharged me. It is a similar feeling to getting released from jail.

The results were good. I had gone from 30 percent breathing capacity to 70 percent. The doctor said we could try and go for more or just hold steady at 70 percent and see how I felt. I elected to just hold steady. I had been through hell and wanted a break from hospitals and surgical procedures. No more trips down the rabbit hole for me. I needed to get on with the life which I had come so dangerously close to losing.

BOB DYLAN

The answer is blowin' in the wind.
—Bob Dylan

I had always wanted to do a reggae CD of Bob Dylan songs. Dylan was a protest singer and reggae was protest music. It seemed like a marriage made in Zion. Dylan had been a big influence on me in my high school years and I knew his lyrics forward and backward. I still remember quoting this verse from "It's Alright, Ma (I'm Only Bleeding)" for a school assignment: "*A question in your nerves is lit / Yet you know there is no answer fit / To satisfy, insure you not to quit / To keep it in your mind and not forget / That it is not he or she or them or it / That you belong to / Although the masters make the rules / For the wise men and the fools / I got nothing, Ma, to live up to.*" These words helped define me—a rebel, and a free spirit to boot.

From my *Reggae for Kids* projects, I knew I was good at identifying the right singers to cover the songs that fit them best—and I was thrilled by the opportunity to present Dylan to reggae audiences. RAS had recently been bought by Sanctuary Records, which was in general a rock-oriented label, so I did not have much trouble convincing them to finance this idea. I had created the whole project in my head. It would be called *Is It Rolling Bob?* (the opening line from the *Nashville Skyline* album) and the cover would have Bob Dylan rolling a big spliff. I worked with the artist Eric White, and this was the only album I ever did where the cover was designed and painted and complete *before* a single note had been recorded.

Soon I began recording some of the tracks for the album. Of course I asked about having Bob Dylan do a Bob Marley song to include on the project. I knew it was a long shot but I figured it was worth a try. If you don't ask, you will never get. I went to Jamaica to record the basic tracks and carefully selected my band. It was Sly Dunbar on drums (who had already played on two of Dylan's albums from the early '90s and had backed many rock artists), Glen Brownie on bass, Robbie Lyn on synthesizers, Steve Golding on rhythm guitar, Chinna Smith and Dwight Pinkney on lead guitar, and Sky Juice on percussion. I sang all the rough vocals so the musicians could lay down the tracks, and I gotta admit I did not do such a bad job.

We recorded fourteen tracks in two or three nights, and I then started to contact different artists about which songs I wanted them to perform. I made CDs of the rhythm track with and without my vocals and presented each artist with a copy of the lyrics so they could go home and study them. I even got the band to tune up so I could ask, "Is it rolling, Bob?" on tape to start the album and leave my mark as producer Bob Johnston had done before me.

198 ❖ THE HALF THAT'S NEVER BEEN TOLD

That week we had the Mighty Diamonds come in and record "Lay Lady Lay." Tabby loved the song and his sweet voice really fit the lyrics. Luciano was perfect for "Knockin' on Heaven's Door," which he changed to "Knockin' on Zion's Door," turning it into a Rasta-inspired gospel-type hymn. The song had already been covered by Glen Washington so Jamaicans were familiar with it, but Luciano really did it up right. And by the time Dean Fraser added his sax, the song was a full-blown hit.

One of my all-time favorite Dylan songs is "The Lonesome Death of Hattie Carroll," which was covered by former Black Uhuru lead vocalist Michael Rose. It was the true story of a black maid living on a Maryland estate who was killed by a drunken aristocrat when his cane sailed through the air and struck her dead. And he was only sentenced to six months in jail. Michael did it so gracefully, and it was especially poignant to hear him—the descendent of a slave—singing Dylan's heart-rending lyrics. A new young singer, Abijah, showed up at the studio and cut "One Too Many Mornings." Billy Mystic voiced "A Hard Rain's A-Gonna Fall," and the great Yellowman struggled with "The Ballad of Frankie Lee and Judas Priest," which never made it onto the release.

One of the major standouts and truly inspired performances was turned in by Sizzla, who was in high demand at the time. RAS had released his first album, and he was managed and produced by Fatis. But now that RAS was owned by Sanctuary, I had to draw up a contract for the deal rather than have a verbal agreement between brethren and brethren like in the good old days. Fatis helped with the negotiations, and this was Sizzla's rare cover song. All his other material was original and radical, as he was a strict Bobo dread and a real hard-core militant. He was going to cover "Subterranean Homesick Blues," which could be considered one of the first rap songs ever released in popular music. I figured Sizzla could rip this song apart, and he did.

He and some of his crew worked the song over before we began the recording. He changed up the opening lyrics from, "*Johnny's in the basement mixing up the medicine, I'm on the pavement thinking about the government,*" to, "*As for those in the basement, marijuana's the medicine and those on the pavement burning down the false government.*" He made other slight changes that gave the song a true Jamaican vibe. When Dylan's manager Jeff Rosen heard the rough mix, I could see in his eyes that he was astounded and knew this album was shaping up to be something beyond what he had expected.

I then had artist Dick Bangham make up cue cards with the lyrics on them so we could film a video similar to the one Dylan had made decades earlier in Greenwich Village with Allen Ginsberg in the background and Dylan flipping through the cards as the song played. The more Dylanesque I could make the project, the better I felt it would succeed with both Dylan and reggae fans. In order to shoot the video in the ghetto of Kingston (without police involved), I had to first meet with the ghetto dons from Maxfield Avenue. Fatis had made these arrangements, as he grew up there and still commanded a great deal of influence and respect. He had vouched for me and these ghetto thugs were sizing me up to see if this white man should be afforded the right to come into their zone and shoot a video. I met up with the dons at a cement-block community center without air-conditioning in the heart of the ghetto—it felt like it was 120 degrees in there. We burned some spliffs together and talked it through, and permission was fortunately granted for us to film the next day.

I had hired a Jamaican crew and bought up lots of food and drinks for all the people of the neighborhood, and we had the streets cleared so we could capture our shot down a lane that was pure Kingston. Pure Jamaica. From Dylan in New York to Sizzla in Kingston. I had Bunny Wailer (portraying Allen Ginsberg) and guitarist Earl "Chinna" Smith in conversation off to the left, just as Dylan had done before. And like Dylan, Sizzla looked nonplussed as he dropped card after card to the ground. The entire video has a surreal quality to it, thanks to the compositional work of the great Dick Bangham, along with the natural talent of the "actors" themselves and the stark ghetto setting, replete with a mangy dog walking through the middle of the shoot.

Later, I grabbed vocal takes with Gregory Isaacs and J.C. Lodge (I wanted to have at least one female voice on the CD, and J.C. and I had worked together many times over the years) at Ariwa studios in London. I also had Don Carlos voice "Blowin' in the Wind" and Apple Gabriel do "The Times They Are A-Changin'" at Lion and Fox in DC. All these sessions (except, of course, the Gregory one) were uneventful with the usual good vibes and the artists performing their best.

I was closing in on completing the recordings but still had a few more songs to knock out. I had selected Toots to sing "Maggie's Farm," which to me was a metaphor for slavery and subservience of not just the body but also the mind. As with the Michael Rose cut, it felt especially meaningful for Toots to be singing Dylan's words; even though slavery was formally abolished on the island in the 1830s, the fact remains that other forms of inequity and mental slavery persist to this day in Jamaica. Like Bob Marley sang, *"Emancipate yourself from mental slavery / None but ourselves can free our minds."*

A few words about Toots: he is the Otis Redding of Jamaican music, and his numerous hits over the decades have earned him the status of superstardom worldwide. He's toured with the Stones and has had the likes of Eric Clapton, Bonnie Raitt, Keith Richards, and Willie Nelson pay tribute to him on record. Also, Toots's longtime manager Mike Cacia and I have been brothers from the early days, from back in the '80s when we used to run around Kingston together, trying to stay out of trouble when trouble came looking for us. And once you are my brother, you're a brother for life—unless, of course, you fuck with me. So don't even try it. Seen? In any case, Toots, now in his late sixties, remains solid as a rock and continues to tour hard—even if he still can't beat me at pool.

So after months of working on the song and memorizing the lyrics (Toots could not read or write), he gave me a call: "Doctor Dread, me ready now. Come make we voice the tune." I flew to Jamaica and we recorded the song and he really put his heart and soul into it. I had my old friend and original Roots Radics guitar player Dwight Pinkney add some wicked bluesy lead guitar to the song and we were done. The result: a real masterpiece and a great accomplishment for Toots. Dylan and

Toots later met on tour in Australia and talked about the song, which I find heartening. Their encounter also underscores why I made this album in the first place: I wanted to explore the intrinsic connection that exists between reggae fans and Dylan fans. Although the two groups are distinct and idiosyncratic, I believe they each have a latent level of understanding and mutual appreciation of the other that I was able to explore through this record.

Another track I knew had to be sung by a specific artist was "Just Like a Woman." And just like Toots is the Otis Redding of Jamaica, Beres Hammond is clearly the Marvin Gaye—and he is beloved by Jamaicans at home and abroad. He had been signed by Electra and I think their idea was to have him cross over to the African American audience, but it never quite worked and he returned to his Jamaican roots. His raspy voice carries so much feeling that he easily gets to the ladies, and he also has the lyrics that can hold the male population, so he has it all covered. A brilliant songwriter, Beres has no problem landing on top of the Jamaican charts time after time. Fatis had produced many of his hits, but Beres was hard to get to even though he said he would record the track.

I decided to leave the twenty-four-track tape with Flabba Holt, the original bass player from the Roots Radics. Respect to Sly & Robbie, the most famous drum-and-bass duo, but in my humble opinion Flabba is the best bass player to ever tear up reggae music. When Flabba hits the bass the whole place is rocking. Since Flabba and Beres were tight, I left it up to Flabba and Jah to work it out and waited to see how things would turn out. It eventually did happen, thanks to Flabba and his persistence. Beres murdered the tune and I love it. Just like I imagined it.

I was friends with Drummie Zeb from Richmond, Virginia, who was playing with Family Man Barrett (the original bass player with Bob Marley and the Wailers, who ironically is reputed to have fathered thirty-eight children at last count). I had told Zeb about my album of Dylan songs and he got excited and said that he had just recorded a version of "You Gotta Serve Somebody." At this point I had all the tunes I needed for the CD, but Zeb had a positive vibe and was excited about this song. He was also good friends with Dylan's bass player, Tony Garnier. After hearing the tune, I thought the song had potential but I wanted the artist Nasio to revoice the track. We also asked Tony Garnier to come down from New York to add the bass line to the song, to bring some more authentic Dylan flavor to the recording. I immediately got a good vibe from Tony. His infectious laugh and good-hearted nature made him an easy person to be around. And with over fifteen years of playing bass with Dylan and his role as Bob's bandleader, Tony certainly had the credentials to be a welcome contributor to this project. Then Dylan's manager Jeff Rosen mentioned that Dylan himself was willing to work on a Marley tune for the CD!

Nasio's manager Steve Weltman agreed to have Nasio voice the tune, but there were a couple of conditions: he had to record in New Jersey, and no one from the label could be present. I had also asked Nasio to change the lyric *"You might serve the devil or you might serve the Lord"* to *"You might serve Selassie I or you might serve the Lord."* I and

I wanted to promote Selassie I as the Second Coming of Jesus, and in the Rasta world we want to rid the world of the devil. Nasio overstood the proposition and went into the studio and turned out a truly magnificent rendition of the song.

As a producer, I always try to capture the vibe of a track. It doesn't have to perfect, but it has to have soul—my mission is to bring out the essence of what an artist is trying to convey. And I believe this is a major reason why people are so moved by music: an artist reveals his or her soul through a medium that enters the ears then goes into the mind and may even get all the way down to your feet and have you dancing!

In Jamaica the harmonica is known as the "mouth organ" and there are not many artists who play it proficiently and even fewer who can get the Dylan sound with it. And since many of the original versions of these songs featured Dylan on harmonica, it seemed necessary to have it in there on some of the tracks. Again Jah stepped in and brought me into contact with Lee Jaffe. Lee was a white American who had managed Peter Tosh, spent lots of time in Jamaica in the early '80s, and played harmonica on Bob Marley's "Rebel Music (3 O'Clock Roadblock)." His harmonica work on this song had earned him a place in reggae music history—a real standout performance. Lee was also a huge Dylan fan and was really pumped up to do this. He tore the songs apart, adding an old-school bluesy/rock-and-roll vibe to them.

Now that all the tracks had been recorded, I went back to Dylan's manager to ask if Dylan had been able to finish up his Bob Marley song for the album. Jeff

Rosen's response was that Bob had tried "Exodus" and two other songs but that he did not feel his renditions were substantial enough, and he would prefer to just let it rest. I was devastated. I who believed all things were possible. In Jamaica they say that "a promise is a comfort to a fool," and I certainly felt the fool for allowing my expectations to get the best of me. So to make up for this, I suggested that perhaps I could do a remix of the Bob Dylan song "I and I," which featured Sly & Robbie on drum and bass. I thought this could be a way to have Dylan on the album; like Malcolm X said, "by any means necessary."

And as things turned out (praise Jah), I and I did come to an agreement that I and I could remix this song and include it on the CD. Sanctuary and Sony worked out the deal, and when I returned from an incredible trip with my family to South Africa, sitting on my desk was a twenty-four-track tape from Sony Music which contained the Dylan song "I and I." I cannot express in words how great I felt, so I will not even attempt such a futile endeavor. Jeff Rosen told me to make sure I took good care of the tape and to get it back to him as soon as possible so he could return it to Sony, and I shared my plans to sell it on eBay and we laughed.

I immediately booked out a night at Lion and Fox and went in to start mixing. When we pulled out the track sheet from the tape, we could see that Sly & Robbie were on there, as well as Mark Knopfler from Dire Straits and Mick Taylor from the Rolling Stones. But most important of all was the fact that HRH Bob Dylan was on there. We started to get a rough mix with the levels on each track to blend, and worked on things like the treble, reverb, and high-, medium-, and low-end sounds. Working and reworking the sonic levels. Rewinding the tape hundreds of times. Sometimes for just five seconds to get one phrase exactly how we wanted it.

Jim and I had learned from over twenty years of recording together how to communicate telepathically. As the mix started to come together and we were putting reverb effects on Knopfler's guitar and had just the right amount of treble on Bob's voice and were bringing out the drum and bass of Sly & Robbie to give the song more of a reggae flavor, I turned to Jim and said, "How fucking great is this? It's three a.m. and we are in the studio mixing a fucking Bob Dylan song. I can't even believe it." It is one of the true highlights of my entire music career and I have to thank John Simson and Jeff Rosen for making it possible. You don't get anywhere in life without the help of others, as no man is an island.

Next Jim and I shifted into another gear for mixing the dub version. Jamaicans had created dub in the late '60s, where the engineer would drop out different tracks and add all kinds of effects like echo and reverb, and turn the song into a spacey, far-out version accentuating the instrumental tracks while sometimes leaving bits and pieces of the vocals in the mix to help bring the listener back into contact with the original song. The dub versions were almost always the B-sides of 7" singles released in Jamaica, and would be played at dancehalls where various rappers would get on the microphone and lay down their own set of lyrics. This is actually what American rap music was born from. And when you are really wasted on ganja, drifting away to the faraway dimensions where dub music can carry you is an auditory exploration that can be quite enjoyable. Of course I would not know this firsthand but have heard about it from some people I trust.

So Jim and I were prepared to totally murder this dub. I had decided to snag Bob's vocal of the word "creation" from the song and echo it out to begin the dub version. And as Knopfler's guitar reverberated in from the beginning and we laid down more of Bob's voice, and when Sly's drum was bouncing all over the room and Robbie's bass would disappear and then reappear, the song started to morph into something that really was out of this world. There's a waterfall in Jamaica that I mentioned earlier where you can swim through these intense falls and into a hidden cave; it is like being inside of a womb. Naturally, I had named the place "Creation." Dub, of course, is a creation too—and hearing that word in Bob's song brought me back there. "I and I Dub" became a true masterpiece and disc jockeys the world over could not believe this was even possible: Bob Dylan in dub. I also produced an equally far-out video for the song with the addition of a theremin track that's also worth checking out.

As soon as the CD was completely recorded and mixed, it was time to put together the cover. I asked my good friend Roger Steffens to write the liner notes. Roger is the foremost authority on Bob Marley in the world—he knows reggae music inside out, and his home in LA is a literal shrine to Bob Marley. He's also the original and longtime editor of *The Beat* magazine, and he had an influential reggae show on KCRW. A child of the '60s who has always lived up to his ideals, Roger wrote an overview comparing Dylan to Marley, and explained how

Dylan's music was simpatico with reggae, and then contributed short pieces about each song. And Roger had also introduced me to Geoff Gans several years earlier.

Geoff had worked on many of Bob Dylan's album covers over the last fifteen years, and was a big reggae fan. He completely got it right. He knew reggae and he knew Dylan, and he mixed all the ingredients together for a perfect recipe that tasted just right. Geoff and I became close for a while and even traveled to Jamaica together and hung out with Bunny Wailer and Fatis. Geoff is the one who managed to do the impossible by snapping a photo of me with the notoriously reclusive Fatis, which I've included in this volume—it's one of my most treasured photographs.

After over a year of hard work, the CD was finally released on August 10, 2004. We got reviews in *Billboard* and *Rolling Stone*, and I was interviewed on NPR, which took the CD to number one on Amazon. Both reggae fans and Dylan fans were digging it. Mission accomplished. We also released a separate CD of all of the dub tracks, which I called *Visions of Jamaica*. And Dick Bangham once again helped me convey exactly what I wanted: the same portrait of Dylan from the *Is It Rolling Bob?* cover, but with some trippy floral tropical plants in the background.

Before long, my friends Seth Hurwitz and Rich Heinecke from IMP (It's My Party) were promoting a Bob Dylan show at Merriweather Post Pavilion in Columbia, Maryland. I had plenty of backstage passes lined up from both Tony Garnier, who was still playing bass with Dylan, and the promoters. Tony had come to see me at my fish job the previous day and picked up a nice whitefish that had just come from the smoker. He asked if he could get another one for Dylan. Later that night Tony dropped by my house to wash his clothes (it is really key to be able to wash your clothes on your day off while on tour), and we prepared a huge seafood feast.

My mom, as well as many of my friends who knew about my Dylan recording, would ask me if I had ever met the man. The answer was always, "No. And I seriously doubt I ever will." But I felt that this night might be different. That the stars were aligning and maybe, just maybe, it would happen. I drove out to the show in my 1960 Dodge Polara station wagon and was escorted backstage and told to park right in front of Dylan's tour bus. A bunch of the band members came out to see the car and I kept telling myself to not ask about meeting Dylan. If it was gonna happen, then just let it happen.

Sitting backstage, a little buzz came through the air as Dylan stepped out of his tour bus and hung with Tony beside the porch. I assumed they were discussing the set list for that night but I noticed Dylan doing a few double takes my way. Next thing I know they waved me over, and Dylan said to me, "You got the best fish. The best music. The coolest car. The coolest hat and shirt. How can all of this be possible?" I thought about it a few seconds and replied, "I guess I am just blessed." We laughed. It felt like we had made a connection. We talked about Jamaica, and my trip there with Geoff Gans. Dylan asked if I could recommend any places for him to visit in Jamaica, which of course I did. He came across as just a normal guy, no pretenses, though he exudes a level of cool that mere mortals can't hope to achieve.

That night I was allowed to watch the show from behind the monitor board on stage-left. The band got into a groove and played an excellent set, with Dylan re-interpreting his songs in new arrangements, as he tends to do in live settings. When he left the stage, instead of heading to his tour bus I was startled to see him making a beeline back toward *me*: he still had Jamaica on his mind, so we had the chance to talk a little bit more. We thumped fists, and as Dylan headed back to his bus I noticed people looking over at me and the shadow of Dylan that had just disappeared.

Shortly thereafter I got a call from his tour manager in Europe asking if I could line up some places for Dylan to stay at in Jamaica. I passed on the information, but I am not sure if he ever made it down there or not. I guess it is probably none of my business and none of yours either. Will Dylan and I ever meet up again? I seriously doubt it. But if the stars and planets properly align, who knows? Maybe Jah does not even know this one. Respect.

ISRAEL VIBRATION

Jah, you're the strength of my life . . .
—Skelly from Israel Vibration

As RAS Records became better established and respected early on, I found that more artists began to come to us directly to release their records. We had signed Gregory Isaacs, Black Uhuru, Inner Circle, Don Carlos, and the list went on and on. Soon I was contacted by Apple from Israel Vibration, who sent me a copy of his solo release *Blue Jeans*. Wiss had also called me and talked about a solo album he did for Jah Life. They both explained to me that they were looking to launch their solo careers and that RAS was the perfect label for them to work with. I had always been a huge fan of Israel Vibration and found their story to be compelling and moving. Their music and harmony style was quite distinctive, and I always looked for originality when signing an artist. And their songwriting abilities and lyrical content also resonated strongly within I.

The three members (Skelly being the third) had all

contracted polio as young children—Jamaica was hit hard with a polio epidemic in the 1950s. As their families could neither afford nor were equipped to raise them with this affliction, they were each sent to the Mona Rehabilitation Clinic up Hope Road in Kingston. There they were well taken care of and had a roof over their heads, beds to sleep in at night, and food in their bellies. They participated in school activities, learning to read and write and play sports. They became friends at an early age, and they took up music through an upright piano at the clinic.

As they grew older they also began to knot up (grow dreadlocks) and give praises to His Imperial Majesty Emperor Haile Selassie I, and took on a more militant position about life and society and the world around them. This did not sit well with the administrators of the clinic and they demanded that these three youths cut their hair and stop with this Rastafari lifestyle. But they had already been singing together and had created a unique type of harmonizing. For the other patients at the clinic, they were very entertaining. But their refusal to back down from their beliefs in Rastafari eventually led to them being thrown out and left to fend for themselves.

They had crutches made from heavy iron pipes to help them walk. But they also had the determination to live and praise Jah regardless of the hardships that were heaped upon them. They settled under a group of macca trees near the clinic, sleeping under the stars on pieces of cardboard. Many of the local residents would pass by and give them food and sit and reason with them. And they would sing of their sufferation and harmonize and soon were known and talked about by the local community. Shortly thereafter they were brought to the attention of noted reggae producer Tommy Cowan, who brought them into the studio to record. And around this same time they were taken up by a Rastafari organization known as the Twelve Tribes of Israel, which found them places to live.

The group decided to take on the name Israel Vibration, and their debut recording for Tommy Cowan, *The Same Song*, became a monster hit for the group. But the success an artist enjoys is not always passed down in the form of monetary compensation, and all three members ended up moving to Brooklyn to see if things would be better for them in America. Eventually the group broke up and they were each pursuing solo careers. And this is when they contacted me.

Their individual recordings were good but nowhere near as strong as what Israel Vibration had done as a group. I explained to them that I would be glad to sign them as a group, and I continually reminded them of how Marcus Garvey had proclaimed that "unity is strength." By working together they could accomplish so much more. The Power of the Trinity. While they were persistent, I stood my ground and eventually they relented.

We arranged to get together at an ital restaurant in Brooklyn. As I had never met them before in person I was very excited the whole five-hour drive up from DC. When I arrived I ordered some food and waited for the brethren to show up. I figured it was a soon-come situation, so I just waited and then waited some more. They never showed. I got in my car again and drove the five hours back home. What else could I do?

When we next spoke they explained to me that they had a show in California and had not realized they would be gone on the day of our meeting. And although I felt dissed, I decided to give it one more try. I had the Roots Radics wrapping up a US tour, so I booked out studio time a few days later. I bought three tickets for Is Vibes and told them if they were serious then they would get on that plane and we could begin recording their first LP for RAS. I was quite relieved (ecstatic, actually) when they all showed up at the airport.

The vibes were set and that night we recorded all nine rhythms for the *Strength of My Life* album. RAS 3037. After I dropped the three men at their hotel that next morning I was on an incredible high. I knew we had just made history. Each one of the Vibes contributed three songs and we had a nine-song masterpiece. The next night I had them come in and put the vocals onto the rhythm tracks. There were rough vocals from the night before but tonight we would record the real vocals.

For the title track, I heard gospel voices in my head. The song started with a cat's meow turning into a lion's roar and was propelled throughout by Nyabinghi drums. Jim Fox brought a local gospel group to the studio and it really made a huge difference—the song was in fact a spiritual hymn. I believe it was the first time that gospel was ever blended into reggae and its results were staggering. Apple, Skelly, and Wiss all took turns singing lead with the other two shifting into harmonies. I knew I could not play favorites as they were all lead singers and each had their egos to contend with, so I had to be careful. No favorites. It is just like with my two sons. I have always told them I love them the same and it is something I always try to live up to.

We called it a day and Skelly, Apple, and Wiss all returned to New York, and my relationship with Israel Vibration had taken a very important first step.

By this time I had an approach to recording that I pretty much stuck to. Vocal phrasing must fit the music, and the lyrics must flow just right to mesh with the melody. So I would frequently suggest changing up lyrics slightly to create a better fit, and sometimes I even wrote whole verses for artists. To me, the voicing of each song is crucial, since it's what most people gravitate toward first—especially for a harmony group like the Vibes. So I would lay down the basic rhythm tracks with rough vocals. I would next lay on the final vocals. Then, typically, I would go to Jamaica and add the overdubs. Keyboards, percussion, vocal harmonies, and horns.

I am not sure if it is a blessing or a curse, but I hear every note in a song. Even the ones that seem to be buried in the mix. It makes me wonder sometimes if I'm even capable of enjoying music like a normal person, after all these years of dissecting recordings track by track, second by second, to try to *feel* the music. Dean Fraser would say that there were always so many sounds and notes swirling around in my head—not just reggae, but everything from classical to blues, from rock to R&B and hip-hop. All swirling around there like in a blender without a lid on it, so the notes just fly out all over the place. And I was able to communicate these sounds to the musicians and we would overdub them onto the existing tracks. Sometimes I liked them once I heard them and sometimes I didn't. And I knew which musicians could get me the licks I was looking for, so I called on them as needed. For the *Strength of My Life* album I brought in Mallory Williams to overdub the keyboards, as I wanted some particularly strong melody lines. And even though Augustus Pablo was a solo artist and would rarely overdub on anyone else's tracks, for some reason he was always willing to work with me and add his melodica to a song or two or more if I requested. His contributions to *Strength of My Life* are amazing. Classic Pablo.

Peter Barry and Mitch Goldberg nailed the cover design (featuring the Hebrew-type lettering with red, green, and gold throughout), and once the record was released, my next step was to tour them and let the world hear this group of brave Rastas who had come together to give praises to Jah through song, to uplift people and give them the strength to know any obstacle can be overcome if one puts his or her mind to it. I had never seen Israel Vibration perform live, and we had a six-week tour of America set up. I rented a Winnebago to take us all over the country; I was the driver, tour manager, and sold merchandise each night.

While I was literally doing the jobs of three people, and had to leave my newlywed wife behind for weeks at a time, I didn't once complain. Being on tour is not easy for either the musicians or their families who have been left behind. Our first gig was for Bill Graham Presents (BGP) in San Francisco. The promoter, Harry Duncan, told me that when it says showtime is eight p.m., the band must hit that first note onstage at eight p.m. sharp. BGP did not fuck around. Apple had drunk some bad blueberry juice and when eight p.m. hit he was in the bathroom shitting his guts out. I was the MC and brought on the Roots Radics to open the show with a few instrumentals to allow the house engineer to fine-tune the sound. When I finally brought on Israel Vibration the crowd went absolutely crazy. Skelly and Wiss both had these heavy crutches to walk onstage while Apple used only a cane. All serious dreadlock Rastas. Each took a turn on the lead mic and the whole thing was very powerful. I found myself in complete awe standing on the side of the stage, overcome with tears.

Ultimately, RAS lost close to $75,000 on the tour, but I knew this had to be done in order to establish the group in the US, and by the reaction I had witnessed firsthand on the road I knew it would turn out to be a good investment. We next toured Europe and had the same response there.

We then recorded the *Praises* LP, and released a dub version of the first two albums together called *Dub Vibration*. I loved putting out dub mixes of the RAS recordings, as it helped to keep the form popular and would also breathe new life into the original recordings—plus, it afforded me a level of artistic control that you can't put a price tag on; not many people can say they spent most of their life having the freedom to do what they want to do. And I especially liked coming up with the names for these newly created dub tracks.

Things with RAS and Israel Vibration went from strength to strength, as they say in Jamaica. While the next major tour lost $50,000, the one after that broke even. The Israel Vibration audience was growing by leaps and bounds, and their fans would buy all their CDs and T-shirts. I had licensed the records to Europe, Japan, and Africa, so they were gaining popularity all over the world. They had such a fascinating story and it was always so inspiring to see them perform live. There was a universal connection made between RAS and Israel Vibration, and they become the cornerstone act of the label and a personal project for me. I respected them as human beings, as they were for me a true personification of Rastafari. There are many people who grow dreadlocks and wear red, gold, and green but do not live by the tenets of Rastafari. The Vibes lived it.

They say that many are called but few are chosen, and I felt I had been chosen for this mission. It's important to note that to Rastas, the first three letters of my surname—Himelfarb—are of utmost importance. In fact, I once received the following letter from a Rasta elder about the significance of my surname:

> Ras Tafari Greetings Doctor Dread,
>   The first time I saw your surname Himelfarb I did notice the "him" and its association with HIM, who is always in I thoughts. I do not want to speculate on the "coincidence," however the reality of the "him" at the start of your surname and other facts about your reality may shed some light on the question. You are a well-known personality in the worldwide Ras Tafari community and have strong bonds and ties in the community. (These are the gentlemen of them that seek HIM.) Through your business and vocation you have played a significant role in the recording, production, and promotion of Ras Tafari music, and cultural Reggae music (directly and indirectly helping to spread the Teachings and the Name of HIM). You have expressed your support for IDOC, a 501(c)(3) nonprofit organization livicated

to promoting the teachings of HIM Emperor Haile Selassie I the First and protecting the rights and interests of Ras Tafari people. You have a close relationship and interactions with Elder Ras Irice, IDOR President, and Elder Baba Ras Marcus, IDOR Treasurer, who are iyahoneers within the Ivine revelation of HIM as the Almighty I and the Ivine language of Ras Tafari. You can check the facts and circumstances of your history and reality. You will know the answer. HIM say, "The harvest of life is character, which grows with time, and it is this factor that determines one's destiny and future." So "him" is in HIM and HIM is in "him."

Is this just a coincidence? I'll let you decide.

When *On the Rock* came out, we had our first real hit with the Apple song "Rudeboy Shufflin'." This was getting major play on reggae shows worldwide and helped take Israel Vibration to a new level. Tours to Israel. To Japan, Brazil, and Peru. France became a huge market for them. We made a great video for the song in Port Royal, Jamaica. All cylinders were firing and RAS was growing right along with the band. Not only financially but in reputation as well.

For the next release I needed to pick a Skelly song to promote as a single, to avoid playing favorites. I chose the song "Feelin' Irie" and we did a very cool video shoot on the streets of Brooklyn. Skelly had become like a don of Brooklyn; he had bought a house there and was firmly entrenched in the community. He was proud to be a Brooklynite and I wanted this reflected in the video. We pushed "Feelin' Irie" really hard and it was Skelly's turn to shine. Mike Malloy had been making high-quality videos for us, which were all shot on 35mm film. Normally these would have cost around $100,000 and up, but Mike made it happen for about $25,000.

We had a major tour booked for Europe to promote the new CD and I went out with them for the first week or two. When we landed, there was a double-decker tour bus waiting, the best you could get. We were getting paid top dollar for our shows and were treated with ultimate respect everywhere we went. I gathered the group and band together and told them that we had made it. That all those years of hard work had finally paid off and here we were. In the moment.

I was so proud to have been a part of the success we had all achieved. Unfortunately, they were absolutely miserable and I could not understand why. Petty politics and power struggles no doubt had seeped into the group. We had been scheduled to do the most popular entertainment TV show in all of France. No reggae artist had ever appeared on this show before, and it would be a big boost for reggae and Israel Vibration. Our two shows at the Élysée Montmartre had already sold out. We were happening. We would perform the new single "Feelin' Irie" on the TV show and kick off this tour on a real high. But they say that one bad apple can spoil the bunch: Apple refused to do the show because he felt we should instead do "Rudeboy Shufflin'," his hit from the previous album. Panic set it, and the show's producers were freaking out at soundcheck since Apple was missing. The band was also clearly off-kilter and not really in it; this was a messed-up situation.

That night in Paris I got really drunk. I am not sure how much I consumed but the whole band, especially Dwight

Pinkney, did not like seeing Doctor Dread in this state. I just sat on the tour bus the whole show and drank and drank and drank some more. Fuck it. All these years of hard work to get to the top and then you want to throw it all away. So many bands have done this and I cannot understand why. Bob Marley had reached the top and remained humble about his insignificance in comparison to the Most High Jah and was able to keep things in perspective. Why can't you see the forest through the trees? Open your fucking eyes. The friction in the group had evidently reached its breaking point and I knew it was only a matter of time before things would seriously fall apart.

After returning home from tour, I remember getting a three a.m. call from Apple from somewhere in Europe complaining that the hotel they were in had bedbugs and that the people there were racist. I told him to work it out with their road manager and asked what he expected me to do from my house in the Washington, DC, in the middle of the night. *Doctor Dread will fix it* became the running joke at RAS.

In an effort to keep the group together, I met up with them in New York City at the "reggae hotel"—a Howard Johnson's on Eighth Avenue and 51st Street with a Jamaican staff where all the reggae artists would stay when passing through town. There were clear differences of opinion and growing resentment between the band members, but it was agreed that we would try to work things out.

Before long I met up with them again in San Francisco, where I found Apple in the hotel lobby berating some innocent young female clerk for being a racist. I was incredibly embarrassed. My mission had been to use reggae to spread the positive messages of love and equality and peace and the beliefs of Rastafari that had brought me under their spell, and here was my most visible group hurling epithets of hate at a young lady. I was not happy. I calmed Apple down and apologized to the woman, but the vibes were all wrong. Wiss, Skelly, and Apple were not talking to each other and onstage there was no synchronicity between them.

Skelly and Wiss complained that Apple took too long when he would sing lead and just keep dragging out his songs. And when the tour bus was ready to pull out at ten a.m. the morning after a gig, Apple would show up at noon. Everyone else would be miserable and vexed. Especially the bus driver. I think Apple did it to prove that if people would wait for him then he must be important. Another night around two a.m. in the middle of Vermont, Apple demanded some red snapper and rice and peas to eat. He blocked my way from getting off the bus and said unless he got his snapper right then and there, I was not leaving the bus. Just picture this situation. It almost came to fisticuffs.

Since none of us ate meat and Wiss was a strict vegan, we all had to address our food needs when on tour. One time in Japan there were these sandwiches backstage and we told Apple to stay away from them. He ate them anyway and found out it was pork and lost his shit. Another time in North Carolina I told Apple to stay away from the cabbage because sometimes they put pork in it down South. He asked the waitress if it had bacon in it and she said no, but I still warned him to stay away. He ate it anyway. When the chef wandered out and said he'd put some of the bacon fat in there to flavor it up, Apple literally threw his plate at the waitress and started cursing her out for lying, calling her an evil white witch and racist and all kinds of other hurtful things. I didn't feel bad for Apple; instead, I felt bad for the people who he abused due to his own stubbornness.

Possibly because he may have been a germophobe, Apple didn't like to use public restrooms, and it got so bad that on the road we'd have to stop the tour bus and find a hotel and explain to the clerk that we needed to rent a room for an hour so Apple could go to the bathroom. Of course, we would end up having to pay for a full night. Those were some expensive shits! One time, as we were driving out from a gig in San Francisco, Apple had to go really bad. It was the middle of the night and he could not wait to find a hotel, so we stopped at a gas station. I had everyone on the bus give him a standing ovation when he was finished with his business. Apple couldn't help but laugh along with us, because he recognized that even though he was a total pain in the ass we all tried our best to put up with him.

Perhaps inevitably, one night in DC, where it had all begun with *Strength of My Life*, everything just fell apart. The band was onstage and went into "Rudeboy Shufflin'," and Apple dropped in the controversial lyric, "*Straight to a guy bumbaclot head.*" Now, *bumbaclot* is just about the worst curse word you can use in Jamaica, and some band members found it offensive. Peter Tosh, at the height of his fuck-you phase, had released a song called "Oh Bumbaclot," which was immediately banned from radio play in Jamaica. *Bumbaclot* and *bloodclot* are fighting words in

Jamaica and you don't throw them around lightly. The argument from some in the band, especially drummer Carl Ayton, was that there were children in the audience at the shows and he did not want any cursing coming from the stage. I believed Apple had the right to use that word even though it had been causing friction within the band—my feeling is that *bumbaclot* is just a word like any other, and it shouldn't be censored, so this was a case where I had Apple's back.

When Apple sang the lyric that night, Carl stopped playing his drums and literally walked off the stage. And then the rhythm guitarist, and the next thing I knew everyone left the stage and the show was over and so was Israel Vibration as we knew it.

Apple left the group, and I think he felt he was like Sting leaving the Police and that a huge solo career awaited him. Skelly and Wiss continued on as Israel Vibration and added two female backup singers to take Apple's place. RAS continued to release Israel Vibration CDs, but it was different now. I was no longer the producer. The Power of the Trinity had been broken. RAS released a solo album from Apple called *Another Moses*; it didn't sell well and Apple faded into obscurity.

Israel Vibration continues to tour but for me it is not the same. Many people ask me if the original lineup will get back together, and all I can say is that they are grown men and need to decide that for themselves. I did assemble a three-CD box set called *Power of the Trinity* where I chose my favorite songs from each individual member and then followed it with an interview. This was my way of getting the three of them back together once more, by creating an immortal artifact that tells the full amazing story of one of the most interesting and powerful vocal trios to ever bless this Earth.

There is so much more I could tell about my experiences with Israel Vibration—Wiss being stuck in Jamaica for two years after testing positive for marijuana, and RAS releasing the CD *Free to Move* once he could come to the US again; trips to Israel, Brazil, and Japan; cornering Tommy Cowan in a room in Kingston and getting him to relinquish the rights to their early music and publishing, for which they had never received royalties. It is all part of the other half.

Many Sunday mornings I still begin my day listening to the song "Strength of My Life," and it is my way of going to church. I often call Skelly and thank him for this great song he gave the world, and he always laughs and tells me he knows how much I love it. Apple lives in Atlanta and is being well looked after by the Peter Tosh estate lawyer Kendall Minter. Wiss is out in Texas so he can be near to his kids. And Skelly is still holding it down in Brooklyn.

And yes, Jah is the strength of my life. For now and for-iver.

FREDDIE MCGREGOR

Freddie, don't you let me waste my time on you . . .
—Freddie McGregor, from the song "Freddie"

When I first met Freddie McGregor I believed he could be the next Bob Marley. Bob had recently passed on and I thought that reggae music fans would be looking for its next superstar. Freddie had all the attributes required to fill this vacancy. He had been recording since he was eight years old when Coxsone Dodd at Studio One had taken him under his wing and nurtured him as a recording artist. Freddie recounted to me how they would give him beer crates to stand on so he could reach the microphone. Studio One was considered to be the Motown of Jamaica, and although Coxsone was a shrewd businessman who did not pay many royalties, most artists who went through school there say they got a serious education in the music business. Freddie's first album for Coxsone, *Bobby Bobylon*, is a true reggae masterpiece.

Freddie is a devout Rasta and a member of the Twelve

Tribes of Israel, a Rastafari organization headquartered in Kingston with chapters around the world—he even traveled to Shashamane in Ethiopia, where His Imperial Majesty Haile Selassie I had donated a portion of his personal land holdings to create a settlement for the repatriation of Rastafari immigrants—in other words, the promised land.

Freddie had a major influence on the early days of RAS Records and my recording techniques. With a knack for writing well-constructed songs with verse, chorus, and bridge all built in, Freddie also had a smooth vocal sound and a strong stage presence. He had the good looks and intelligence and ambition that made his chances for success in the music business a very real possibility. I made the decision to back him 100 percent.

But Freddie was also a hustler. In Jamaica, as in many other parts of the world where people struggle to survive, I and I need to do some juggling to help make ends meet. It is just a way of life. The cops take bribes, some people sell weed, idealistic politicians get into office and then line their pockets, and so on. And it is not always illegal. It could just mean having a little business on the side to supplement the meager salaries doled out by most employers. Anyway, I picked Freddie and Freddie picked me. We were in it together.

After delivering the second release for RAS Records, *Come on Over* (RAS 3002), which I later found out was an album that Linval Thompson had produced, Freddie and I began a series of studio recordings where I really learned the ins and outs of being a producer and working with musicians. It started with RAS 3009, *Across the Border*. I learned how to record the basic tracks first. How to then lay down the vocals and harmonies. Next, to overdub the other instrumentation, usually keyboards, to enhance the sound and fill in any gaps. Finally, to add the horn sections before beginning the mix on the full twenty-four-track tape. I saw Freddie's approach to recording and learned that being a producer is about spending as much time in the studio as possible, and observing and using your ears to guide you to the sounds you are looking to create. Night after night with total absorption in the music.

In order to introduce and promote Freddie to the American public, I began touring him frequently in the US with a package of artists with Freddie as the headliner. All backed by the Studio One Band. This was now known as the RAS Posse, and it was responsible for getting the label established with disc jockeys, journalists, and reggae fans across the country. As I worked to spread the Real Authentic Sound of Jamaican reggae from coast to coast, the hard work started to pay off. I had finally realized my vision of creating a music label where the artists worked together with me for our mutual benefit. Without the artists, you have nothing, so treat them right and hopefully they will do the same for you. This is the foundational philosophy upon which RAS was built.

Freddie and I became very close during this time and we even cowrote a few songs together. Musically, I feel the album *All in the Same Boat* was the pinnacle of the work we did together. The production quality was extremely sophisticated for reggae, and it had some pop elements that attracted the attention of Polydor Records in London. And although RAS still had another album due from Freddie, we allowed him to sign a deal with Polydor since the advance was so large and it might have been his only chance to get a big break in the music industry. Regardless, Polydor dropped Freddie when his album failed to get the response they hoped for. Fortunately, he was able to rebound with a few albums he did of classic Jamaican reggae songs for VP Records.

Freddie was a smooth operator and he knew how to work the system and keep his career going. He never sold tons of records and never drew huge audiences, but he was good enough to stay in the game. He also contributed great songs to our *Reggae for Kids* series, one of which featured his eleven-year-old son Stephen doing a rap called "School Done Rule." I paid Stephen his first royalty check.

Freddie took his money from the Polydor deal and built Big Ship Studio in Kingston, and many years later Stephen would become the producer in residence there. Freddie also had a daughter with Judy Mowatt named Yeshemabeth who also became a reggae singer. And with Freddie to help guide their careers, the kids had a good role model to look up to. Stephen became one of the hottest producers in Jamaica and was soon laying down rhythms for Sean Paul and other popular dancehall artists. And since everyone was now looking to Stephen for rhythm tracks, Freddie and I talked about how these might generate some big publishing monies. We decided that Tafari Music would administer the publishing for Stephen and the rest of the McGregors—I came up with the name Tinkentoe Publishing (after the pungent stinkin' toe fruit) for their company.

The songs we registered were mostly compositions

230 ◆ THE HALF THAT'S NEVER BEEN TOLD

from Stephen (who was now dubbed "Di Genius") and it felt like the early vibes of Freddie and I working together had rekindled and the fire was burning brightly again. But shortly into the relationship I started to hear grumblings from the Freddie camp, and Freddie became harsher in the way he talked to me. The next thing I know we received a letter from EMI informing us that they were contesting the control of all Stephen Mc-Gregor compositions. I was furious. I felt like such a fool to have believed Freddie was being genuine in wanting to work together. As usual, it was all about the money.

Our contract stated that we had the first right of refusal if anyone else offered them a publishing deal. It seems that Sean Paul's manager had made Stephen believe he would be much better off with EMI and that they could give him a big advance. Of course they could: they were the largest music publishing company in the world. So with complete disregard for our agreement, EMI proceeded to make their own deal.

Freddie and I had the harshest conversation in our personal history. I told him he was the same little tief who had ripped off Linval Thompson so many years before, and I hung up the phone on him. For years I refused to listen to Freddie McGregor music and his very name was verboten in our home. This same brethren who played for over four hours at my wedding would do me that. I could not believe it. But money has a strange way of making people behave in a certain manner, and Freddie fell into that trap again and again. A real hustler.

I next saw him at the funeral for Gregory Isaacs in Jamaica and he smiled at me from his car, but I wanted nothing to do with him. I then saw him in California

when he and Bunny Wailer performed at the same festival, and again I would not acknowledge his presence.
But one thing I have learned from Jamaicans over the
years: it is okay to get vexed with someone, and then you
let it go and things can revert back to how they were.

I have now started enjoying Freddie's music again
and have no ill feelings toward him. Whatever karma
he created will be taken care of by Jah the Almighty.
It is not for me to hold onto. When I next see Freddie
he'll know I've let everything go. In any event, along the
way I realized that he could never be the next Bob Marley. No one can. Those were just immature beliefs from
someone new to the reggae business.

GONDWANA

Escucha mi gente, el reggae está llegando . . .
Listen up, my people, reggae is coming . . .
—Gondwana, first lines from the first song
of their first CD, *Together*

O ne day, out of the blue, Oscar Sayavedra from
BMG in Chile called to tell me about a group
called Gondwana that wanted me to produce
their debut album for the label. They had been listening
to the music I produced for Israel Vibration and were
inspired by my work. Of course I was interested. Any
chance to visit some exotic part of the world was always
a temptation. I explained that I first needed a tape of
some of the rough recordings, as I did not like to just
take people's money if I could not make a true commitment to their project. I ended up being very pleased
with what I heard. Especially the lead vocalist. And the
offer to fly me first class and pay me $10,000 put the ic-
ing on the cake I was getting ready to eat.

Upon arrival I breezed through customs and spotted

a contingent of dreadlocks waiting for me. My Spanish was pretty good from all those years I spent in South America, so I was able to easily communicate with everyone in the group. Only the lead singer spoke any English. We all hit it off immediately.

I joked with them that when the customs officers asked me the purpose of my trip to Chile, I told them I had come there to murder the past dictator Augusto Pinochet. I was sensitive to what had happened in Chile back in the early '70s. The Chileans had a democratically elected Marxist president, Salvador Allende, but he'd been overthrown in 1973 with the support of the CIA, as America wasn't comfortable having a Communist in power. Pinochet was brutal; he had Allende killed and rounded up the opposition. America often represents its support for democracy, and sometimes we even go to war to ensure it for other nations. Yet in Chile, and in other countries where we don't approve of who has been democratically elected, we have too frequently undermined their sovereignty. The CIA organized truckers in Chile to stop the transport of food to its people, and as Bob Marley says, "a hungry man is an angry man." The people got angry, Allende was overthrown, and Pinochet was entrenched in power.

In 1970s Chile under Pinochet, you could get arrested if you had a beard. Imagine that. Arrested just for having facial hair, you fucking Commie leftist piece of shit. Many people were taken away to the country and became "the disappeared." In fact, the percussionist Don Chico of Gondwana, who was a very hard-core and serious Rasta, had both of his parents murdered by the Pinochet regime. His parents were poets and free-thinking people, and Pinochet considered anyone like this a threat to his power. Pinochet was still alive and living in Chile when I arrived there, so my joke about coming there to kill him sparked many a conversation about America's complicated relationship with democracy. Don't get me wrong—I love this country, and I don't take for granted our hard-fought freedom; in some other places, I'd be locked up for even writing this type of shit. But a key question that isn't asked often enough is *Why?* Why do terrorists feel compelled to kill innocent people? By treating symptoms and ignoring the underlying problems, we'll never stop the violence and get to the root of what's bringing on this abhorrent behavior.

Gondwana was the name of the Earth before the continents shifted and broke apart. When the world was one. If you look at Africa and South America you can see how they once fit into each other as a single land mass. So the name signifies oneness and unity. I liked it.

The sessions in the studio went extremely well. It was like we were having a party with jokes and laughing and eating cherimoyas, and I am not sure I ever had a better time recording an album. None of the members had ever left Chile and they treated their guest Doctor Dread with maximum respect. I think some of the newspaper articles and TV stories had me mistaken for Dr. Dre, which I thought was pretty funny.

In one song where the horns sounded like some drunken barroom brawl as everything deteriorated and people shouted in the background, I suddenly smashed two beer bottles together. Perfect timing and the perfect sound. Years earlier I had smashed two Heineken bottles together at Philip Smart's studio in Long Island for the Don Carlos song "Spring Heel Skanking." Philip was bent out of shape because there were shards of glass all over the his studio floor, but sometimes if you need a sound, then you just need a sound. The song "Irie" ended with me asking in a loud voice, "Is it irie?" and about thirty people responding with a loud "Irie!" In the song "Smile Souling," which was written in English by the bass player I Locks about his young daughter Souling, we brought the girl to the studio to voice the words, *"Daddy, I love you."* She is over twenty years old now but that line still sounds as sweet as can be. The song "Armonia de Amor" ("Harmony of Love") was the hit of the album and had the excellent line, *"Tu cuerpo es un poema de sensualidad"* (*"Your body is a poem of sensuality"*).

We had many invitados (guests) appear on the album since this was as much of a celebration as it was a recording. Great harmonica players, many talented vocalists, and even a tuba player who happened to stop by the studio. We became very close in that week of recording and I grew especially tight with Quique Neira, the lead singer, who is one of the most genuine and positive people I have ever known. The great vibes I and I created for these recording sessions were a major factor in our ability to capture the true magic of the music.

As we wrapped up, I was showered with gifts and, of course, lots of cherimoya fruits that I liked so much. Before leaving the country, I explained to the group (in Spanish) that regardless of how popular they became and how big this album got, they must remain humble lions.

The CD, once again mixed by Jim Fox, was released

to great fanfare in Chile in 1998. The youth embraced Gondwana and the message they were putting forth. Red, gold, and green started to be seen all through Santiago, and dreadlocks became more common. Soon Gondwana was selling out stadiums and the CD went multiplatinum there. A reggae movement had been born in Chile, and I loved how it was pure roots reggae with a positive message and a revolutionary spirit. I had seen in Jamaica how the reggae movement had shifted away from the music that Bob Marley and many of the roots reggae artists like Burning Spear had brought forth in the late '60s and early '70s, toward dancehall lyrics extolling gangsterism and misogyny.

Quique explained that he could not even walk down the streets without being mobbed, and that reggae was taking over Chile. I felt so good for the group. With all this new fame, Quique had turned inward and was reading his Bible seriously and looking for knowledge from within. This was the best news I could hear. Many entertainers take their popularity and become obsessed with public adoration, but Quique had instead chosen the inner path.

RAS decided to release the CD in America and Europe as *Together*, and I think it is one of the best reggae albums ever recorded. I also believed that with Gondwana I could expose Latinos to positive roots music and help raise the consciousness of a new generation, which seemed ready for positive vibes in a post-Pinochet landscape. When I believe in something I always have to give it a try, regardless of whether I fail or succeed. I just have to do my best, which is the most I can do.

In traditional RAS style, we released a dub version

of the *Together* CD, called *Phat Cherimoya Dub*, resplendent with beautiful cherimoya photos. In fact, the running joke was that I would be paid in cherimoyas since I seemed to prefer them to money.

Following the great success of the first album, I was asked to come back to Chile and produce Gondwana's second record. I wanted to build on the momentum we had created and try to reach for higher levels, with an eye toward the international Latino market. It was a different studio this time but the vibes and songs were all good, and things proceeded in an upful and positive way. There was still lots of joking and guests, but the process was a little more serious this time. The band had gotten a taste of success and now they wanted to make sure the next course would be as tasty as the first. It was a more methodical and carefully executed project, but the music was tight and everyone was pleased with the results.

We mixed the album in DC, and although it did not have the same cosmic eloquence as *Together*, it still had a number of great songs and one ballad I knew would be a hit. I decided to name the CD *Second Coming* and put a large portrait of His Majesty Emperor Haile Selassie I on the front cover. Not only was I making a statement that Haile Selassie was the Second Coming of Jesus, I was also suggesting that real roots reggae was now coming from outside of Jamaica and that the world should take notice. I was very pleased with this CD and wanted the band to make a step beyond their own country to see how the world would take to them. Aside from mixing some tracks in Washington, DC, the band members hadn't really seen the world outside of Chile—and this was a golden opportunity to open them up to the next level of global overstanding.

I was very close with the top reggae promoters in Puerto Rico and I gotta give a shout out to Victor and Annibal from Cool Runnings, who became good friends and always treated the artists right. When it came to reggae, they ran things in Puerto Rico, and roots reggae is what the youths there were craving. And the people loved Gondwana—a roots reggae group singing in Spanish was a cross-cultural connection that resonated deeply in Puerto Rico. We started our tour there and traveled next to Washington to perform, did a show with Burning Spear in Baltimore, went to New York to SOBs, and then flew to California for more concerts. They played at Reggae on the River in Humboldt County in California, and they got to hang out under the redwoods, smoke some sinse, go for a swim, drink pisco sours, and meet the likes of Bunny Wailer and other reggae luminaries. It was a joy to make these connections, and Gondwana loved every minute of it.

Since I'm a born troublemaker, when we got to LA I decided to play a joke on my brother Doug, who was living there at the time. During one of our late-night drunken sessions, the musicians and I were discussing the worst curse words you can say to someone in different languages, and we agreed that *"chupa me"* ("suck me") is the most insulting phrase in Spanish. My brother was excited to meet the band and see their show, and I told him that they didn't speak English but were all great guys. I told him that in Chile, it's customary and polite when greeting someone to put out your hand and say, "*Chupa me*." Of course, he then went one by one to each band member and put out his hand and said, "*Chupa me*," just like I had told him. The musicians knew me well enough to appreciate my twisted sense of humor, though my brother wasn't quite as understanding when I explained to him later that he had just told each musician to "suck me." I still laugh when I think about how fucked up it was to do this to him.

Though the California gigs were not as well attended as I would have hoped, we had one last great adventure before Gondwana headed back home to Chile. I had booked flights for all of us to go to Jamaica beforehand. I knew this would blow their minds. To go to the root of where all this great reggae music came from. To experience Jamaica firsthand with Doctor Dread at the controls. I could not think of a greater gift for Gondwana. To feel the Jamaican culture and get to know its people and its tropical beauty.

We went to Kingston and spent a few days in and around the city and then headed over to Port Antonio. I wanted them to experience both the city and country vibes. We visited some studios. They met some artists and other friends of mine. In Port Antonio we would go to the beach or hike up Reach Falls in the Blue Mountains. I knew I had helped open Gondwana's eyes to the world and it would give them a better overstanding of life. A gift upon which no price tag could be put.

Oscar Sayavedra was still managing the group and taking very good care of them, setting up shows in places like Mexico and Argentina. The world was opening up to them. And after a while it was time to do a third album.

There was some tension growing in the band as Quique and the bass player (and original founding member) I Locks were having some issues. I Locks owns a cool reggae club in Santiago and is a wicked bass player but was not as deep into Rastafari as Quique. The band informed me they wanted to do the next album at a studio owned by Jon Baker in Port Antonio, Jamaica. Geejam Studio had just recorded some tracks by Gwen Stefani's band No Doubt and had a good reputation building in the industry. It felt like both a vacation and a recording project, with everyone digging the vibes of being in Jamaica again and recording there.

I also wanted to take the guys back to Kingston so they could get a better feel for the big-city energy. In Jamaica, though I loved the sunshine and beaches, I actually spent far more of my time in the recording studios of Kingston, the creative heart of the country. So I booked out some studio time and arranged for Don Carlos to add some vocals to a track called "Jamaica Jam" that we had cut in Port Antonio. Then I brought in Dean Fraser to touch it up with his rollicking sax. It was an authentic Jamaican-Chilean collaboration, and I wanted the band to feel that they were on equal footing with the local music community.

Other notable tracks included the happy number "Felicidad," along with "Te Recuerdo Amanda," which is a popular song originally written and performed by the Chilean folk singer Victor Jara, whose music I was introduced to by Gondwana. Under Pinochet's iron-fisted rule, Victor Jara was thrown in prison as an "enemy of the state." The prison guards broke his fingers with the butts of their rifles before ordering him to play his guitar. When he picked it up and tried to strum it with his busted fingers, the guards shot him dead. Point-blank, in cold blood. Pinochet was later convicted of crimes against humanity by an international tribunal in Spain, and although he is now gone, he is not forgotten.

Though I did my best as a producer and tried to keep the energy positive, in truth the album, titled *Made in Jamaica*, was a downhill slip musically. Sometimes you just accept the cards you are dealt and make the best of it. The group broke up shortly after the album's release. I Locks kept most of the members together and they continue to tour as Gondwana. I recently saw them perform in Virginia and Oscar is still with them and says they are doing great business in Mexico and Europe. They have a lead singer with long dreadlocks, and I Locks is still playing wicked bass, but I miss Quique. He comes to Washington now and again to mix his solo recordings with Jim Fox and we always get together and have him to our house for dinner. He is still pure and has such a positive spirit and my family and I have much love for him. He always calls me Doctor and I know he is a lifelong friend. Jah guide and protect you for-iver, Quique. Un abrazo.

THE FISH BUSINESS

These are the big fish who always try to eat down the small fish . . .
They would do anything to materialize their every wish . . .
Woe to the downpressors, they'll eat the bread of sorrow!
—From "Guiltiness" by Bob Marley

After the two stents had been inserted into my pulmonary arteries so I could breathe again, and after losing my job with Sanctuary Records when they sold the company, I needed to start looking for work. A job. I had spent the last twenty-five years in the music business, had no college degree, and was not really suited to work an office job. I had a small music label, Tafari Records, but it was not earning money. I still did some touring with Bunny Wailer and made good money this way. But as I described earlier, the final straw for me came when Bunny canceled a long-awaited Brazilian tour. It was a crushing blow and I realized my days of touring Bunny were over. One week later I would apply for a sales job in the seafood business.

I had been in this business with my brother thirty

years earlier, and I knew quite a bit about fish (as I had given up eating meat and pork decades earlier). I had noticed some seafood trucks moving around town and liked the logo of Profish. I got on the phone and told the owner I was the number one seafood salesman this city had ever seen, and after he explained that I might possibly be number two (after him), an interview was set up for the following week. I met with the two owners, Greg Casten and Tim Lydon. We talked and I gave them my pitch and they bought it and said they would give me a shot.

It felt strange to change my profession at fifty-four during a time when the US economy was in bad shape and jobs were tough to find. I started at a salary of 25 percent of what I had been getting paid at Sanctuary. That was a tough pill to swallow but I needed a steady income, and most importantly Profish offered health insurance for my entire family. I also knew I would have access to the best seafood and would literally be putting food on the table for my family each night.

My first day at work was torture. I was in a cramped and stinky office in a DC ghetto, with junkies and alkies hanging around the street where our warehouse was located. I tried to keep my cool and stay focused on work but I had a major panic attack. I was freaking out. I had no idea what in the world I was doing there. I wanted to run out the door and never come back. What the fuck was I thinking? I knew I could not make it in this environment.

When I got home that night I was trembling. My sister-in-law Julie explained that most people in the world go off to their jobs every day and just make the best of it so they can pay their bills and get on with their life. That I had been living the dream and my years in the music business were an aberration and that very few people in society ever had the freedom I'd experienced. She said to hang in there. Get up and go to work the next day, and slowly things would settle in and I would be okay. She was right.

Things gradually got better, and as the new kid on the block, I was enthusiastic and working hard to learn the business and get accounts. I even called some chefs I had sold fish to thirty years earlier and got some positive reactions. I began to build up my sales, but I also learned what it meant to work for The Man. To be a part of the dog-eat-dog world where everyone is trying to claw their way a little higher out of their pit. Even the sales guy sitting next to me said that it was "every man for himself."

This concept was foreign for me. I had always believed (and still do believe deep to my core) that if you do good work and take good care of people, it will come back to you in the form of both money and positive vibrations. With music, I figured that if I produced a quality product that people liked, customers would buy it and money would flow back into the company. Why should it be any different with fish? My modus operandi was to only give my customers good product so they knew they could depend on me and would continue to order. Yes, price was a factor, but just like in the music business my strategy was to build strong relationships with chefs where they could trust me to take care of their needs. I wanted to network and build a reputation that Gary was the go-to guy they could depend on for their seafood.

It was tough. Many of the chefs liked to beat you up and make you feel like they were doing you a big favor by buying fish from you. A mini-power trip within their own small universe. By demanding to see how far you would go to have the honor of selling to them. As I was just getting started, I had no choice but to do whatever was asked of me. And in the year and a half I worked at Profish, I was only once told that I was doing a good job. That was when I had doubled my sales from one month to the next. The company would post all of the salespeople's results on a spreadsheet so everyone could see, and I guess they thought if they created a competitive atmosphere it would make everyone work harder. I also spent a lot of time with the guys in the warehouse and cutting room since I spoke Spanish, and they appreciated this. They made sure my customers got the best fish, and they would also take good care of me when I was bringing home fish for my family.

One morning we had gotten a new shipment of flounder and I sold a bunch to an important DC seafood market. I casually asked the owner Tim what we paid so I would know what to charge my customer. Instead of giving me a simple answer, he barked at me to go look it up on a computer. I had noticed how Tim always berated everyone who worked there and seemed to enjoy being a dick just to be a dick. Most of the people there disliked him, as he rarely showed any respect for his employees.

I was learning how the Babylon system (which Peter Tosh famously called the "shitsdem") worked firsthand, which I had of course heard about in countless reggae songs, but had never really experienced since I'd always worked for myself. The labor system is too often based on control and power, replete with time clocks and the threat of punitive action. This company's oppression was palpable, and permeated every aspect of the organization. But Tim had pushed me one too many times and I was going to defend I-self. I told him that no one could disrespect me or anybody in my family. No one. He told me to get out of his face in front of a bunch of employees and I refused. It got to the point where he just left the office and headed out into the warehouse. I followed him out there to continue our conversation. I told him to go ahead and fire me. Right then and there. (I had asked the same thing of the majority owner Greg Casten some months earlier, which he had refused to do; I had started to believe that my time at work was hell and that being fired would be my salvation.) Tim looked really nervous. I'm not sure if anyone had ever stood up to his bullying. As he walked away again, without firing me, I continued to vent.

It's funny, but some of the Latino workers came up to me that day and shook my hand and asked if they could help me load fish into my car. They actually thanked me for standing up to the boss, and more than one of them told me I had big cojones. Even the sales guys saw a different side to Gary Himelfarb, and they now knew that I should not be messed with. Yet I am not a quitter, and I hung in there and tried my best to do a good job.

But a few months later there was another incident and Tim finally told me I was terminated. I put out my hand and thanked him. I really did. I gathered up my shit and left. Free at last. Free at last. As it turned out, Tim ending up serving a number of months in the slammer for purchasing illegal striped bass. There were strict regulations about fishing for striped bass in the Chesapeake Bay, whose population had been dangerously reduced over the years. But the greed of some cannot be abated, and it's money alone that motivates how some people choose to live their lives. The company was fined close to one million dollars. This had all gone on long before I started working there but had been hanging over Tim and the main fish buyer the whole time, and maybe that was the reason he was such a miserable son of a bitch.

So, I was briefly out of a job but soon found work with Congressional Seafood, one of the area's best seafood distributors. I was told I would need to come to work at five a.m. because that is what everyone in the market did. The crews worked all night to get the fish cut and ready to put onto trucks for early-morning delivery, and the salespeople needed to be there to handle the phones and enter orders. My salary was significantly less than what I had been making at Profish, but they had the upper hand. I believed that once I got in there they would recognize my value and compensate me accordingly. We talked and joked and they said they'd hire me just so I could get them tickets to concerts, but I wanted them to realize what I could bring to the table; I explained that I did more than just merely sell fish. At Profish, I had created publicity for the company and streamlined some of their more cumbersome systems; I wrote a biweekly newsletter about the company to circulate throughout the industry; and I built important relationships with chefs. With me, they would get more than just a salesperson.

I also knew the long hours were going to fuck with my arrhythmia, since lack of sleep is a major factor, yet I had no real choice. Without a regular paycheck from another source, what else was I going to do? Even during my first meeting with the company, the arrhythmia hit me hard and I was just barely able to keep it together.

Wow. Dragging my sorry ass out of bed each morning around four a.m. was not what the doctor had ordered. It really kicked my ass. Many of my friends told me how proud they were of me—I had changed my whole life-style to work in the fish business just so I could support my family. And I knew my family was relieved that I was working again. That said, I will admit it was tough and that I became a more miserable person because of this; the conditions, both physical and mental, were wearing me down.

I was so tired by the time I reached home each afternoon that I would just drop from pure exhaustion. I would wake to have dinner with my family and often I would cook the fish I brought home, as I was getting pretty good in the kitchen. To me, cooking is like a science—each food reacts differently under certain conditions and when combined with other foods, just like the elements in the periodic table. A leek will behave differently if sautéed in oil at high or low heat, or depending on when exactly it's put into a dish, or on the size of the cut.

As soon as dinner was done, the chefs would call me to order their fish for the next day. I had gotten the reputation as the one sales guy who stayed up past eleven p.m. So I was essentially working from four a.m. till eleven p.m. If the phone rang with fish questions I would answer it. It's just part of being a salesperson.

I managed to push my schedule back a couple of hours, but the conditions were still intolerable to me. I could not even think straight. I loved to eat seafood and I felt good about working with chefs, but I found the working environment there distasteful. Imagine after all the freedom I had experienced in the music business and the open-mindedness of the artists I worked with to have to show up each day at the cold, smelly fish market and face these conditions. The love I had felt from the Rastafari community was nowhere to be found. Just the insatiable drive to make money and maintain a hierarchy where those at the top persecuted those beneath them.

We had this rough-and-tumble guy from Philly named Ritchie who ran the warehouse. We never hit it off; he didn't like my style and I didn't like his. He once accused me of "sucking dick" when I was assembling an office chair for one of the VPs. Then he asked me if I would be "sucking the dick" of a different VP when we would be driving three hours to New Jersey to land a big account. I later took him aside and explained I found his dick-sucking references extremely distasteful and told him to stop. But he did it a third time and I really blew up. He tried to apologize but I did not want to hear it. Imagine having to work in this type of environment where people cannot even have the respect to treat you like a human being. It was something I and I faced every day. Every fucking day.

In Jamaica, when two people meet they will often bump fists and say, "Respect." This means that I will respect you and you will respect me, and this level of mutual respect fosters a healthy relationship. I had al-

ways tried to express this basic principle in all my interactions with people in the music business and in my life
in general, but clearly the rules of the game are different
in the corporate world. Respect means nothing; the only
motivating principle is money. How many people working today loathe their jobs and the people they work for?
How many people feel exploited by their bosses, or not
adequately appreciated or compensated for their hard
work? I had been lucky and privileged to have never been
beholden to anyone before this point in my working life.
But can you blame people for resenting their jobs when
they work for greedy motherfucking hypocrites and are
required to be subservient? (Believe it or not, I was literally told to be "subservient" in boardroom meetings
with my employers.) Later, I couldn't help but reflect
upon the parallels between the corporate world and the
slavemaster mentality.

I continued to hang in there and did the best I could.
For me, it was all about sales. Why should the company
care what I do or where I am as long as I'm delivering strong sales? But they did. Most companies want to
own their employees. To keep you down. If you become
too powerful, you become a threat. These guys were
extremely confrontational and seemed to take pleasure
in the misfortunes of their competitors. Instead of ap-
preciating the hard work of their employees, they were
aggressive with no empathy for anyone but themselves,
walking around the place like Nazi storm troopers in-
flicting their will over others. I could never understand
this approach. Where was the kindness? Where was the
love?

Soon my time in the fish business was over. I was

fired for reasons I cannot get into, and it did not resonate well with my family. But I had served my five years
and in my mind I was done. My last words to one of the
bosses were, "Until you start caring about other people
and not just about yourself, you will always be in pain."
I had promised to let him know the secret of why he was
always in pain once I left the company, so I took this opportunity to tell him.

I had come into the job believing that the meek
would inherit the Earth and that by being kind and generous to people, all would be repaid. And when I left I
saw that greed and power and the thirst for money was
what controlled the Earth. The meek did not stand a
chance. It was a wake-up call that deeply disturbed me,
though what could I do about it?

I knew that my days of working for The Man were
behind me. That I would need to reinvent myself on my
own terms. I will tell you that I and I am trying very
hard and it is a daily struggle but I will never give up.
That Jah is still my light and salvation and His will and
my hard work will get me to where I need to be. Jah
live!!!

AFTERWORDS

As it was in the beginning, so shall it be in the end.

Wow! What an incredible feeling!!! To relive all these events of my lifetime and put together these fourteen songs for your listening pleasure. Yes, each chapter is like a song for me. And I appreciate that you have taken the time to listen.

My friend Mike Watson from midnightraverblog. com (a very good writer in his own right) told me at lunch recently that my purpose in writing this book was to document my legacy. I disagreed with him but he continued to push his point—and I guess you can say he was right. To share with you some of my experiences and what they have taught me. Clearly, the half I have told still leaves another half that is untold, and so it shall remain.

Today, as I approach sixty, I have many interests that keep me busy. After living through the contraction of the music business, I have now launched a Caribbean food company. Inventing new products to excite the palates of people around the world while at the same time promoting the positive aspects of Jamaican culture, in the same manner as I did with RAS and my mission to spread positive reggae music. And somehow, again with the grace of God, the music and food are now working together to carry one another to higher heights.

But what is most remarkable to me is that my publishing company, Tafari Music, has been reunited with RAS Records by virtue of a worldwide publishing deal I have made with BMG, which recently purchased the RAS catalog. Ras Tafari. Together again, and with Doctor Dread at the helm of the ship. I and I know that only Jah Almighty could have made this happen. There is no other explanation.

They say the gift of God is eternal life, and I have come to believe that we have children who in turn have children, and so on, and that a part of us remains alive for-iver in the spirit of our offspring. As I watch my youth grow into men I can see how life does go on and nothing really remains unchanged.

I have always left it in Jah's hands to set before I my destiny, knowing that I must do my part to ensure that I can achieve my goals while at the same time having faith that Jah does protect I and I. My life has been a blessing and whatever else is in store for me will come and I will always give thanks.

Jah guide and protect you all,

Doctor Dread

I AND I GIVE THANKS

Give thanks and praises to the Most High,
Give thanks and praises so high . . .
—Bob Marley from the song "Give Thanks and Praises"

There are so many people to thank that this really is an impossible task—I don't even know where to start. I know many people might expect or want to be included in my book as they have been a real part of my life through the crossing of our paths. But since I have met such an enormous number of people in my life, I could never mention everyone. Sometimes people come up to me at shows and get all excited and say how good it is to see me again, and I really have no idea who they are. It makes me uncomfortable, as I and I know we all are one, but the database of my brain is just not capable of remembering every person I have ever met. If I overlooked you or forgot to thank you, you can still consider yourself thanked. Seen?

So first of all I want to thank my editors at Akashic Books: Ibrahim Ahmad and Johnny Temple. I did actually write this book myself and didn't just have it recorded and then transcribed by someone else. But the book is significantly better now that Ibrahim and Johnny have made their corrections and tightened up some of the syntax and been the arbiters of what should stay and what should go. Roger Steffens and Mike Watson also read my chapters as I completed them.

Now to the list (in no particular order): Amy "Night Nurse" Wachtel, Manijeh Mavastian, Marz Attar, Lisa Remeny, Dick and Linda Bangham, Kelly Lee, Jody Callen, Lauraine Bacon, Vince DiMella, Juan Harris, Shaka, Barry Wright, Mercedes Hughes, Raymond Paris, Derrick Parker, Anthony Acinapura, Carol and John Bruno, Patrick, Jon Sabban, Packy Malley, Karen Small, Lenox, Negus, Buffy, James Lee, Kevin Maines, Teresa Diehl, Smitty, Lyn Reittenbach, Pasta, Kevin Kinsella, Lisa and Peter Melmed, Claire Lerner, Courtney Poulos, David Baram, Holly Fraser, Carl Palmer, Pat Chin, Brother Jack, Iris, Sidney, Jake Homiak, Maxine Stowe, Jon Baker, Yvette, Rose, Mikey Dread, Dermot Hussey, Steve Parelman, Yannick Cam, Al Bunetta, Peter Bunetta, Nina Simmons, Dylan Neymour, Patrick Blackwood, Dan Feingold, Sean Dwyer, Mark Dickenson, Steve Cornwall, Tommy Noonan, Bas Hartong, Mike Jason, David Miller, Nicole Wilkins, Melody Serecki, Bill Nowlin, Duncan Browne, Jah Mikes, Susan Piver, Tarrus Riley, Chronixx, Mike Caplan, Pauline Hill, Peter Schoonhoven, Justin Engels, Joy Ellington, Richard Hermitage, Rootsman Kelly, Pat McKay, Byron Whitely, Dera Tompkins, John and Elise Simson, Victor Cruz, Annibal, Russ Vaughn, Warren Smith, Ana Avital and Jahved, Susan de Leon, Jah Cure, Mary Steffens, Lloyd Evans, Tom "Papa" Ray,

Barrington Levy, Johnny the Dentist, Tom Silverman, Mike Malloy, Style Scott, Macasea, Sky Juice, Robbie Lyn, Asher Brissett, Selwyn, Ronnie Butler, Cleveland Brownie, Dalton Brownie, Danny Brownie, Everton Carrington, Yami Bolo, Annette Brissett, Bunny Brissett, Kim, Foxy Brown, Ras Sam Brown, Asher and Sharon, Cedric and Yvonne Myton, Chaka Demus & Pliers, Tappa Zukie, Orly Marley, Peason, Peashead, Desi, Steve, Robin Armstrong, Winston Riley, King Jammy, Scorpio, Alvin Ranglin, Leggo, Simon Buckland, Ruffy & Tuffy, Wayne Jobson, Terry Currier, Ayoola Daramola, Marcia Griffiths, Gussie Clarke, Lancelot, Keith Porter, David Isaacs, Winston Jarrett, Ini Kamoze, David and Noelle Kirton, Little Lenny, Little Kirk, Patrick Roberts, Simeon Stewart, Ron Zealans, Paul LaMonica, Peter Schwartz, George Michalow, Ric Bracamontes, Shaggy, Sean Paul, Sharon Burke, Ronnie Burke, Tony Johnson, Earl Chin, Ken Williams, Sarge, Papa Wabe, Tony Carr, Pat McKay, John Blake, Lisa, Bobby Newby, Ricky Hillocks, Prince Malachi, Jesse Royal, Errol O'Meally, Sugar Minott, Scientist, Desmond Williams, Half Pint, Tony Rebel, Queen Ifrica, Carol Rose, Sister Carol and Dean, Cocoa Tea, Sanchez, U-Roy, Prince Jazzbo, Eddie Lee, Byron Lee, Junior Marvin, Chris Govinda, Familyman Barrett, Yvad, Justin Engles, Bert Pipers, Taylor and Trent Branson, President Obama, Noel Alphonso, Justine Ketola, Gretchen Smith, Andrew Baron, Joy Ellington, Melanie 9:30, Renee Schapiro, Donna Westmoreland, Jean Houza, Pam Ginsburg, Ed Stack, and all the many others I have forgotten to mention. You know who you are.